Charles

# THE COTSWOLDS

# THE COTSWOLDS

Text by
MICHAEL HALL

With photographs by
ERNEST FRANKL

THE PEVENSEY PRESS
Cambridge England

*Front cover* Eastleach Martin: the church, founded by Richard Fitzpons, one of William the Conqueror's knights. To the left of the tower is the 14th-century north transept with windows in the Decorated style, unusual in the Cotswolds. In the foreground water plants edge the River Leach. The churchyard is full of snowdrops in early spring

*Back cover* Burford Church: wall tablet (1689) to Sarah, daughter of Richard Bartholemew, beside the east window of the south chancel chapel


Published by The Pevensey Press
6 De Freville Avenue, Cambridge CB4 1HR, UK

Maps: Carmen Frankl

The assistance of Miss Monica Eardley-Wilmot, Miss Ursula Knatchbull, Dr M. E. Smith and Mr Eric van Tassel is gratefully acknowledged

Edited by Ruth Smith

Designed by Tim McPhee
Design and production in association with
Book Production Consultants, Cambridge

© Michael Hall, Ernest Frankl and The Pevensey Press, 1982

ISBN 0 907115 07 1 hard covers
ISBN 0 907115 08 X paperback

Typesetting in Baskerville by Westholme Graphics Ltd

Printed in Hong Kong


This book is also published as part of a larger book, STRATFORD-UPON-AVON AND THE COTSWOLDS, available in hard covers and as a paperback.

# Contents

# CIRENCESTER STREET PLAN

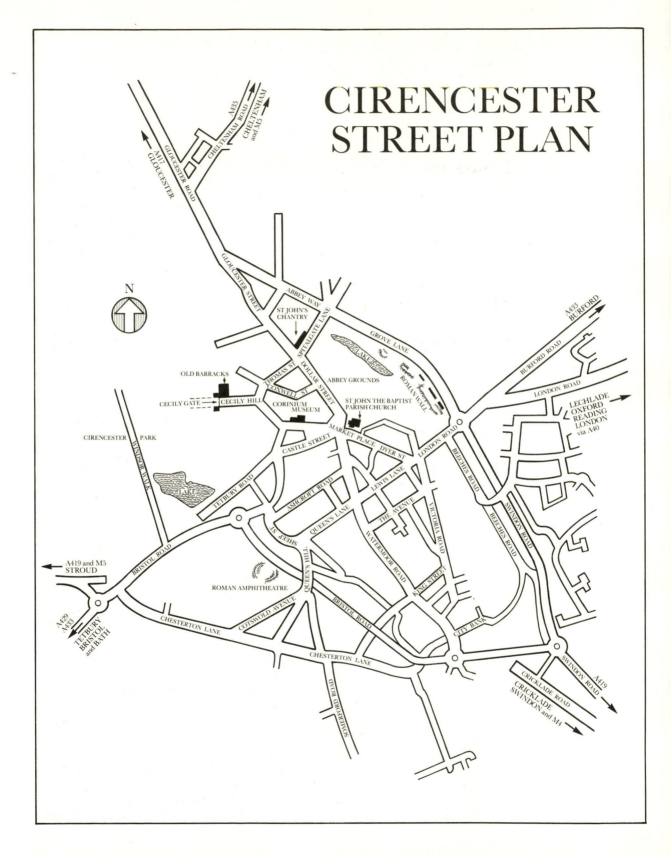

# The Cotswolds: an introduction

The belt of limestone which crosses England from Portland Bill to the Humber is at its widest and highest in the Cotswold Hills. Here it has tilted to the south-east, producing on the west a steep scarp slope rising sharply out of the Gloucester plain and the Vale of Evesham, and on the east a gradual slope falling away into Oxfordshire. The Cotswolds have no exact boundaries (in this book they are taken to cover the area shown in the map at the end of the book), but they lie mostly in Gloucestershire. They possess two distinct landscapes, both famed for their essentially English charm: in the west steep hills and gulleys, often thickly wooded, and towards the east the exposed uplands and the gentler valleys of the Cotswold rivers, the Churn, Coln, Leach and Windrush. The area is unified and given its characteristic beauty by its stone. The limestone is called 'oolitic', i.e. 'egg-stone', because under a magnifying glass the closely packed grains of carbonate of lime deposited around tiny specks of sand resemble the roe of a fish. The best limestone, called 'freestone' by the quarrymen, is a superb building material, easy to carve when newly quarried but hardening on exposure. It is variously coloured, depending on the presence of limonite, an iron mineral: in the west, especially round Painswick, it is silvery grey; to the north and east it becomes golden, even orange in the case of 'Guiting' stone from Coscombe, near Stanway. Whatever the colour, it attracts lichens which vary its textures and hues and intensify its ability to glow in the sun, apparently retaining light. These characteristics have been appreciated by many architects: Sir Christopher Wren chose stone from Taynton and Upton, near Burford, for the interior of St Paul's Cathedral; Guiting stone was used for Melbourne Cathedral, Australia; and Cotswold stone is the material of many of Oxford's finest domestic, university and college buildings.

The availability of local stone is one of the main reasons for the distinctive Cotswold vernacular architecture, in which the domestic style of the 16th century is perpetuated because it makes such good use of its materials. A typical Cotswold house has prominent gables, a low steeply pitched tiled roof with dormers, casement windows with stone mullions and transoms, and a moulded drip-course round the tops of the windows and doorways. These traditional forms have a practical purpose: limestone is very porous, so the roof must be steep to let the rain run off quickly; and a dip in the roof prevents the tiles from shifting. Tiles are the traditional Cotswold roofing material. Though they are often called 'slates' they are not slate in the geological sense but are made from pendle, thin fissile limestone which is left on the ground after quarrying so that frost freezes and contracts the thin films of water ('quarry sap') lying in layers within the stone. A hammer-blow can then split it into tiles, which are hung on the roof in graded courses, the biggest at the eave and the smallest on the ridge. Cotswold tilers use 26 sizes and have a name for each, e.g. Long Wivutts, Middle Becks and Short Bachelors. Pendle is now no longer quarried, so for traditional roofs on new buildings tiles from demolished buildings are sold

— at such high prices that some people sell their old roofs and replace them with artificial tiles, depriving ancient barns and cottages of their beauty and swifts of their nesting-places. The traditional style lapsed in houses of mansion status when classical architecture was fashionable in the 17th and 18th centuries; renewed interest in vernacular forms in the next century caused it to be revived even for great houses. Barns (of which there are hundreds of ancient examples, many larger than the village church) and cottages remained unaffected by fashion.

The other traditional building skill that still flourishes in the Cotswolds is dry stone walling, practised for thousands of years and especially after the enclosure of agricultural land in the 18th century. It is simply a method of building walls by laying stones on top of each other: they are roughly knocked into shape but no mortar is used, though modern walls are often capped with cement; traditionally the wall is finished with a row on end. Usually the stone is just picked off the ground nearby or quarried in narrow strips at field-edges. The art is to position each stone so as to secure the best fit; the grain has to lie as it did in the ground, or the stone will flake in frost. A well-made wall can last for centuries.

The limestone and its soil help to determine the vegetation and wild life. The Cotswolds were probably once entirely deciduous forest, with beech the dominant tree. Clearance began in Neolithic times, and today dense beechwoods survive only on the western edge, notably round Birdlip, and even these are not in their primeval state. Cranham Wood in particular is famed for its botanical richness. The Cotswolds are well known for their limestone flora: the pasque flower (mostly to the north), small scabious, large wild thyme, marjoram,

*▲ The varied hues and textures of weathered Cotswold stone and the lichens it attracts: a detail of the exterior of Stanton church. The angel is a modern addition, an example of the constant care and restoration most Cotswold churches have received through the centuries*

birdsfoot trefoil (locally called 'butter and eggs'), bee and fly orchids, and horseshoe vetch, the essential food of the larvae of chalk-hill blue and Adonis blue butterflies. Local rarities are the Cotswold pennycress, found in quarries, and the limestone woundwort, now confined to the neighbourhood of Wotton-under-Edge, the musk orchid, common in the Cotswolds, but rare in Britain as a whole, and red helleborine, scarcely known in Britain outside the Cotswold beechwoods and very rare there. Glow-worms abound, for they feed on small snails which are plentiful in lime-rich soil. Large white edible snails are common in the woods – contrary to popular belief, they inhabited Britain long before the Romans. The quarries harbour large populations of the lesser horseshoe bat and colonies of the much rarer greater horseshoe bat. Foxes are numerous and much hunted; fallow deer run wild in the woods; important research into the life of the badger has been carried out at Rendcomb Wood. Several pairs of buzzards nest in the central Cotswolds and the hobby, a small rare falcon, is occasionally sighted.

Humans first left traces in the Cotswolds c6000 BC. They were hunters and gatherers whose flint arrowheads have been found to the south. The first farmers and herdsmen were Neolithic immigrants (c3500 BC) who started systematically clearing the forest. About 85 of their long barrows, or burial chambers, are known in the Cotswolds, and constitute one of the most important concentrations of Neolithic monuments in the country (many of them, however, have been spoiled by careless excavation, and more have been lost beneath the plough). Each consists of chambers walled and roofed with massive slabs of stone and enclosed by a cairn, a mound of stones which is usually 30–60 m

▼ *A fine example at Weston-sub-Edge of a typical Cotswold limestone house, with all the essential features of the local style – prominent gables, a moulded drip-course round the tops of the windows and a beautiful roof of Cotswold stone tiles (notice the dip in the roof, which prevents the tiles shifting)*

long and up to 4 m high and now covered by vegetation. Many were enlarged for successive burials, and some were used for over a thousand years: centuries later they kept an aura of sanctity and attracted legends still told today. The best surviving excavated examples, both accessible to the public, are Hetty Pegler's Tump, near Uley, and Belas Knap. Bronze Age peoples built round barrows, but by comparison with (for example) Wiltshire there are few in the Cotswolds – Wyck Rissington has one – which suggests that the Cotswolds were less colonised in the Bronze Age. The most striking monument of this period in the region is the circle of standing stones at Rollright, erected *c*2000 BC near a Neolithic tomb. The longstone on Minchinhampton Common and the Tingle Stone in Gatcombe Park are examples of isolated Bronze Age monoliths. 17 Iron Age hill forts on the edge of the escarpment, whose steep valleys were ideal for defence, show that this area was heavily populated *c*800 BC, and unfortified settlements of the same date have been found at Lechlade and Fairford. *c*AD 1 the Cotswolds were conquered by the Dubonni, Belgic tribesmen who established their capital at Bagendon in the Churn valley.

When the Romans conquered Britain they made the Cotswold uplands their frontier (*c*AD 47) and created a military camp at Corinium (now Cirencester). Being near an important road junction – the end of Akeman Street (from St Albans) at the crossing of the Fosse Way (from Bath to Leicester) and Ermine Street (from Gloucester to Silchester) – Corinium grew rapidly, and once the frontier moved north it became a civilian city, the second largest in Britain, in which Roman and British ways of life intermingled. There were also important Roman settlements at Bourton-on-the-Water and Coln St Aldwyns, and numerous villas, probably mostly owned by Romanised Britons. The best

▼ *Bibury in winter: a characteristic terrace of simple Cotswold cottages, given distinction by their building materials – Cotswold limestone and tiles. In the foreground is a dry stone wall, representing one of the oldest building traditions of the region – here capped with cement in the modern fashion*

▲ *Spring at Coln St Aldwyns: the Coln in flood. The Coln's gentle valley, like those of other Cotswold rivers, the Windrush, Churn and Leach, encloses some of the loveliest scenery in the Cotswolds and some of the prettiest villages in England*

known and best preserved of these is at Chedworth; the site at Woodchester has one of the finest Roman mosaic pavements in England, showing Orpheus charming the animals with his music. There seems to have been a school of mosaicists at Corinium specialising in the Orpheus myth, a story which later acquired Christian overtones. The few signs of Roman Christianity in the Cotswolds include a graffito acrostic, now in the Corinium Museum, Cirencester, which when unscrambled reads 'A Pater Noster O', and the Chi-Rho sign, symbolising Christ, scratched on the nymphaeum at Chedworth to Christianise a pagan shrine.

Corinium's public buildings were maintained for a time after the Romans left, but by the late 5th century the town and most of the villas were deserted. Saxon settlement was a long and often bloody affair: the local kings were finally defeated in battle at Dyrham in 577. The Saxons made the Cotswolds a province of the kingdom of Mercia called Hwicce, lived in existing settlements, and used the Roman roads. As the predominantly Saxon origin of their names indicates, most present-day Cotswold villages already existed by the time of the Norman Conquest. Cirencester did not regain its former importance because it was too near the kingdom of Wessex to be useful as a capital for the Mercians. Instead Winchcombe became the centre of local government and continued so after the disappearance of Mercia, when the Cotswolds became a separate county, Wincelcumbescire: they were not absorbed into Gloucestershire until the 11th century. Struggles between Mercia and Wessex were common. A battle in 752 was subsequently commemorated every year at Burford until the 18th century by a Whitsun and midsummer procession, in which a golden dragon (the emblem of Wessex) was paraded through the streets. Christian influence was strong by the end of the 7th century, when Ethelred of Mercia granted land for the foundation of a monastery at Withington. Much of the Cotswolds rapidly passed into the hands of religious communities, which encouraged and grew rich on sheep farming and the sale of grain. Cotswold wool may have been used in cloth exported to Europe as early as the 8th century. The Saxon monasteries at Tetbury, Withington and Bibury disappeared before the Conquest, but Bibury's Saxon minster church survives, much altered and enlarged. Other churches with notable Saxon features are at Coln Rogers (a Saxon nave and chancel), Duntisbourne Rouse, and Daglingworth, which, besides a pre-Conquest south door and sundial, has four impressive Saxon sculptures.

At the time of the Norman invasion transport was by the Roman roads or by the salt ways running from salt-producing Droitwich in Worcestershire through the Cotswolds to Lechlade, Cirencester and Chipping Sodbury. These remained the major routes throughout the Middle Ages. Arable farming was still the chief source of income. With increasing wealth markets quickly became established during the early Middle Ages. Cirencester, the only market in 1066, flourished once more because of its closeness to main roads, and soon replaced Winchcombe as the Cotswolds' most important town. New markets were at Lechlade (the highest navigable point of the Thames), Burford, Moreton-in-Marsh (on the Fosse Way), Chipping Campden and Wotton-under-Edge (which had to be refounded in 1253 after the town had been burnt to the ground). Limestone began to be used on a large scale for building and the wool and cloth industries expanded, causing the disappearance of villages as more

▼ *Hetty Pegler's Tump, near Uley, a Neolithic long barrow, one of the best preserved of the many burial chambers erected in the Cotswolds 3000–1800 BC. The entrance portal is c1 m high. The mound was first excavated in 1821; about 15 skeletons were found inside, with evidence that the barrow had been used for interment in Roman times*

and more arable land was turned over to sheep-runs.

The Church, the chief owner of this new wealth, built extensively, producing one of the most glorious concentrations of Norman village church architecture in England. Elkstone is outstanding; it has a superbly carved south doorway and sculpted tympanum, and a stone-vaulted chancel – a rare feature that also survives at Hampnett and Avening. Of the many richly carved doorways Quenington's are the most spectacular; Windrush has especially good beak-head ornament. Boldly carved tympana can be seen at Ampney St Mary, Dowdeswell, Harnhill, Little Barrington, Lower Swell and South Cerney. The best fonts are the very different examples at Rendcomb and Southrop. Fragments of an exquisite 12th-century wooden crucifix at South Cerney are a reminder that this profusion of Norman sculpture is a fraction of what existed in these churches before the religious controversies and iconoclasm of the 16th and 17th centuries.

Sheep were farmed in the Cotswolds in pre-Roman and Roman times and archaeologists have found traces of Saxon looms; but it was only in the Middle Ages that the wool industry in the Cotswolds, as elsewhere in England, replaced arable farming as the chief source of income. British wool was the finest in Europe, and Cotswold wool was reckoned second only to the much rarer Lemster Ore of Hereford and Shropshire. Cotswold sheep, descended from stock imported by the Romans, were noted for their large size, long necks and thick white wool. Many of the Cotswolds' great barns were built to store wool, such as the one at Stanway, built for the Abbot of Tewkesbury, and Arlington Row at Bibury, which was later converted into weavers' cottages. In the later

*▲ The tympanum over the south door of Elkstone church, an example of the wealth of Norman architecture in Cotswold parish churches, shows Christ in majesty, with God's hand above, surrounded by the emblems of the evangelists and (left) the lamb of God. It is framed by a row of beakheads, varied by a figure leaning backwards and clutching the snouts of his neighbours, and two ordinary human heads (the donors?)*

11

Middle Ages cloth was exported rather than wool, as the duty to be paid on it was less. Most of it was white broadcloth, sent to Antwerp to be dyed and finished, although there was also some trade, later to be very important, in coloured cloths – duns, olives and the famous scarlets and blues in particular. The earliest physical traces of the cloth industry are the fulling mills – one that stood at Barton, Temple Guiting, was the first in England (1185). (Fulling consists of soaking and beating the loose mesh produced by the weaver so that it shrinks to become cloth.)

Wool made a fortune for the Church: 'as sure as God's in Gloucestershire' is a medieval saying which may have wry undertones, for three-fifths of the Cotswolds were in the hands of a Church as notable for its wealth as for its piety. In 1066 there were four great landowning Benedictine abbeys on or near the Cotswold borders, at Malmesbury, Gloucester, Winchcombe and Eynsham. In 1107 Henry I refounded the monastery at Cirencester, giving it to the Augustinians and starting a long history of ill-feeling between the monks and the townspeople, for no abbot could resist meddling in town government. Between 1246 and 1251 Richard, Earl of Cornwall, expended huge sums of money on a new Cistercian abbey at Hailes. After his son presented the abbey with a phial of Christ's blood in 1270 Hailes became one of England's most important places of pilgrimage. The great periods of medieval Cotswold church architecture were the 12th and 15th centuries, when the wool and cloth trades were at the height of their prosperity. But there are also some good examples of the Early English style, with its lancets and 'stiff leaf' ornament (late 12th–13th centuries), as at Wyck Rissington and Eastleach Turville. The Decorated style

▲ *Doves on the capitals of the chancel arch at Hampnett church: one of the best examples of Norman sculpture in the Cotswolds. Like the rest of the chancel, they were painted c1871 by the rector, the Rev. W. Wiggin, in an attempt to recreate the appearance of a medieval church*

(13th–mid 14th centuries) coincided with a slump in the cloth trade (partly due to the Black Death), and its characteristic flowing window tracery and ball-flower ornament are rare in the Cotswolds: the west window at Ampney St Mary and the south transept at Minchinhampton are splendid examples.

The boom in the cloth trade in the 15th and 16th centuries also made the fortunes of individual merchants: John Tame at Fairford, Thomas Fortey and William Midwinter at Northleach, the Cely family and William Grevel at Chipping Campden and, earliest of all, 'Dick' Whittington, three times Lord Mayor of London, who acquired large parts of Stroud and the surrounding countryside in 1395. Most were unable to buy large estates for themselves because so much of the Cotswolds already belonged to the Church, and many spent their money on their local churches, which rival the great wool churches of East Anglia as triumphs of Perpendicular architecture and monuments to the wealth and piety of England's clothiers. The Tames rebuilt Fairford church, donating its famous stained glass, and helped to rebuild Rendcomb and alter Barnsley. The Forteys partly rebuilt Northleach; William Grevel – 'the flower of the wool merchants of all England', according to his memorial brass – gave money to Chipping Campden, rebuilt by later merchants; at Lechlade John Twinyhoe added a chantry. The marks or symbols of these men were carved and painted all over their new churches, on corbels, in glass, on brasses: John Tame's, for instance, on the exterior of Fairford church tower, appears with emblems of trades allied to the woolstapler's – the glover's gloves and shears and the tailor's open scissors. A clothier wove his mark into the cloth he made; a reputable mark was highly prized and frequently bequeathed in wills.

*▼ One of the many impressive ancient barns of the Cotswolds, with the characteristic steeply pitched tiled roof; this example is on the estate of Sudeley Castle. In the apex of the gable are pigeon-holes: pigeons were formerly important as a source of fresh meat in winter, and many dovecotes can be seen in the Cotswold villages – one of the most interesting is at Naunton*

At the Reformation the huge ecclesiastical estates were broken up, and though sheep farming was not reduced there were many more small flocks. Almost every landowner had sheep, and throughout the 16th century there were probably never fewer than a million sheep in the Cotswolds. Markets lost their importance as farmers increasingly sold their wool direct to the clothiers and as the cloth trade shrank, though as late as the early 18th century 20,000 sheep were sold at Stow Fair.

The cloth industry began to contract in the mid 16th century, causing wealthy clothiers to divert their fortunes into the land they had acquired after the dissolution of the monasteries. Many of the Cotswolds' famous manor houses – Stanway, Upper Slaughter, Bibury Court, Hidcote House, Ablington Manor and others – were built with fortunes made in the cloth trade. The Thirty Years War closed traditional outlets on the continent, completing a shift of the diminished industry from Cirencester to Stroud. Here it prospered: there are many mills in the area dating from this period, e.g. Salmon Springs near Stroud (1607) and Egypt Mill near Nailsworth (1698), and numerous large houses with attics designed to accommodate looms. 17th-century wool merchants generously endowed almshouses, schools and hospitals, notably Lady Dorothy Chandos at Winchcombe and Sir Baptist Hicks at Chipping Campden.

During the Civil War Charles I's headquarters were at Oxford, and the Cotswolds became strategically important (the battle of Edgehill (1642) was fought on their border). Early in the war the king commandeered the cloth-producing areas to clothe his troops, but the Parliamentarians had garrisons at

▲ *Upper Slaughter Manor, built for the Slaughter family in the 16th century, is one of the finest Cotswold Tudor manor houses and typically gives the impression of being rooted in its landscape, its steep gables peering over the rise in the ground*

Bristol, Gloucester, Malmesbury, Bath and Cirencester itself. In January 1643 Cirencester repulsed an attack by Prince Rupert, but the following month, after some of the garrison had left to help capture Sudeley for Parliament, it fell. The prisoners were locked in the church and, according to tradition, their friends broke the stained glass windows in an unsuccessful attempt to release them (although in reality the loss of the glass seems to have been due to centuries of neglect). They were taken to Oxford where, in return for a pardon, their leader, Colonel Fettiplace of Swinbrook, promised they would never again bear arms against the king. But Cirencester was soon recaptured, and the Parliamentary governor of Gloucestershire, Colonel Massey, seized eight Royalist garrisons in Oxfordshire and Gloucestershire, including Beverston Castle, in 18 days. The last Royalist army in England was defeated at Stow-on-the-Wold in 1646, after a bitter struggle in the market place. Nor was this the last civil bloodshed in the Cotswolds: in 1649 Cromwell suppressed an insurrection in his own army at Burford. The rebel soldiers were locked in the church for the night, and one carved his name on the font: 'ANTHONY SEDLEY PRISNER 1649'. The next morning they were taken onto the roof to see the three ringleaders shot in the churchyard. Many of the great landowners preserved their inheritances in the face of sudden political change with considerable ingenuity, though not all went as far as Lord Saye and Sele of nearby Broughton Castle, who spent the Protectorate on Lundy Island to avoid signing Charles I's death warrant. John Dutton, a woolman's son, persuaded Cromwell that he had been forced into his staunch support of the king, and busied himself building Sherborne Manor. Lord Herbert (grandson of the Marquess of Worcester, who had given enor-

▼ *A Cotswold village street: Stanton, on the steep north-western edge. This village, built from local golden limestone, owes its particularly cared-for appearance in large part to restoration by the squire, Sir Philip Stott, an architect who bought the estate in 1906*

mous sums to the Royalists) gained Cromwell's favour and kept part of his property by abandoning Catholicism and calling himself Mr Somerset. After the Restoration he prospered again: he was created 1st Duke of Beaufort and inherited Badminton, where he began to build the greatest house in the Cotswolds.

The cloth industry flourished once more in the 18th century, the home market having become as important as the European. Stroudwater scarlet was the cloth used for soldiers' uniforms and hunting pinks; Uley blues, almost as famous, were material for the finest coats. The secret of the dyes, closely guarded, was reputed to be the softness of the water, but in fact the water of the west Cotswolds is hard. What really counted was the experience of the weavers and dyers, who judged the strength of the dyes by tasting them. The most renowned manufacturer of Uley blues, Edward Sheppard, built himself a country seat 2 miles east of Nailsworth, at Gatcombe Park (now the home of Princess Anne and Captain Mark Phillips). Many lesser clothiers were also sheep-rearers and built substantial farmsteads scattered over the Stroudwater hills. Sheep farming was the predominant industry until the mid 18th century, despite attempts to diversify. In the 17th century commercial tobacco growing was tried near Winchcombe, but it was suppressed by the government to protect the plantations in the American colonies, and dragoons burnt the crop in 1667. Cottagers continued to grow it for their own use, and mothers who could not afford breakfasts for their children would give them pipes to smoke instead. By the end of the 18th century Cotswold agriculture had become largely agrarian: on the uplands miles of newly erected dry stone walls broke up the vast medieval sheep-runs into small fields. The 'high wild hills and rough uneven ways' complained of in Shakespeare's *Richard II* took on their familiar

▶ *A wealthy medieval wool merchant's home: Grevel House (late 14th century) at Chipping Campden, built for William Grevel. The impressive two-storied bay window is adorned with gargoyles*

▼ *The source of the Cotswolds' early wealth. Cotswold sheep, Britain's largest breed, were reared for their heavy fleeces, which earned them the name of 'Cotswold lions'. The forelock is traditionally left unshorn. During the decline of the local wool trade in the 18th century the breed was replaced by smaller, quicker-fattening sheep, and today only a few hundred remain; this one was photographed at the Cotswold Farm Park*

delightful chequerboard look – an effect that is most pronounced in late summer, when the fresh stubble and the burnt contrast with green pasture, ripened corn still standing and fields already ploughed.

The cloth industry had a dramatic boom at the beginning of the 19th century: over 200 mills were erected between 1800 and 1825. It was already overmanned and now become chronically so (partly because of an influx of unemployed soldiers after the Peace of Amiens), with low wages for its workers in consequence. Large unplanned weavers' settlements spread up the steep slopes, as at Bussage, Chalford and Eastcombe. Spinning and weaving was done in the cottages; the cloth was taken to the mill for fulling, and then dried and stroked with teasel heads to raise the nap. Teasels were cultivated in the Cotswolds for this purpose until the 20th century; they are difficult to grow but even today no adequate substitute has been found (the ones used now come from Somerset). The nap was then shorn – originally with hand shears, but after 1815 with a rotary cutter, which inspired Edwin Budding of Stroud to patent the first lawnmower in 1831. Finally the cloth was dyed, hung in the fields to dry, repeatedly shorn and brushed, and given a glossy or damp-resistant quality by hot pressing. All the workers, even children, rose at 4 a.m. and worked until 9 or 10 p.m. Though the advent of mechanisation did not provoke widespread violence (as it did in Wiltshire), it caused desperate anxiety. Paul Wathen, a mill-owner who lived at Lypiatt Park, received a threatening letter from his shearmen: 'Wee Hear in Formed that you got Shear in mee sheens and if you Dont Pull them Down in a Forght Nights Time We will pull them Down for you We will you Damd infernold Dog'. The worst disturbance was at Wotton-under-Edge, where several rioters were killed and troops were called in (1825); the vicar of Uley installed a bell in his church to summon the dragoons in case of trouble.

The Cotswolds' canals were created to serve the cloth industry. The Stroud-water Navigation, linking Stroud to the Severn (completed 1779), was joined to the Thames by the Thames and Severn Canal in 1789, opening up a large market for the produce of the Stroud valleys and providing a route to London for the manufactures of Birmingham and coal from Staffordshire. The Thames and Severn had 44 locks and one brilliant piece of engineering, Sapperton Tunnel, but within a few months of its completion the new Oxford Canal had created a shorter route between London and the Midlands and drastically curtailed its trade. It was closed in 1933. The Stroudwater Navigation, which did better, closed in 1941. The coming of the railway also harmed the canals. Brunel built two railway tunnels in the Cotswolds, at Sapperton and at Box. The latter, nearly 2 miles long, was the most ambitious of its time and its construction cost a hundred lives.

Suddenly the cloth industry collapsed. In 1838 only 15 of Chalford's 41 mills were working. This was partly because the Cotswold streams were not powerful enough to enable the mills to compete with the volume of cloth produced in Yorkshire. But even given other sources of power, the industry would not have been able to support so many mills, and bankruptcies were inevitable. At Uley a thousand workers lost their jobs when Sheppard's mill closed. Many emigrated, there being little else to do. Weavers could not go to church for want of decent clothes; their families lived on water and salt for breakfast, and potatoes and fat for supper. Mill-owners who had enough capital to diversify started making tweeds and shawls, but in Dursley and Wotton-under-Edge the industry was

*▲ Chipping Campden market hall (1627), in the market place beside the High Street, where one of the Cotswolds' busiest markets used to be held. Financed by the local magnate Sir Baptist Hicks, it was intended for the sale of butter, cheese and poultry. Left is a corner of The Martins, one of the town's finest 18th-century houses*

dead, and there were never again to be cloth mills north of Stroud. The deserted buildings were gradually taken over for light engineering works or by firms making carpets, paper or furniture. Today woollen cloth is produced only by two firms, which still make Stroudwater scarlet for soldiers' tunics as well as cloth for a variety of purposes – industry, clothing, the baize for billiard tables and the uniforms of the Vatican's Swiss Guards (the demand for footmen's liveries has declined somewhat). There are only five working mills where once there were more than 200; they make the same amount of cloth annually as the Cotswolds produced in 1841.

The Cotswolds spent most of the second half of the 19th century poor, rural, remote and unvisited. The market towns of Chipping Campden, Minchinhampton and Tetbury, once so busy, were silent and decaying. Agriculture remained profitable for large farmers but many small landowners went under: even the Duke of Beaufort had to sell land. One of the first books to popularise the region, *A Cotswold Village* (1898) by J. Arthur Gibbs, the squire of Ablington, counterpoints lush descriptions of Cotswold beauty with accounts of the barren and deserted countryside in which he pursued his favourite pastime, hunting: 'Now that farming is no longer remunerative, the whole country seems to be given up to hunting. Depend upon it, it is this sport alone that circulates money through this deserted land.' He was right about the economic importance of hunting, and even today many people around Badminton would lose their livelihood were the Beaufort Hunt to be abandoned; but he was already wrong about the desertion of the Cotswolds.

In 1871 William Morris, famous as the founder of the firm which had revolutionised Victorian decoration by a return to medieval models, rented the Elizabethan Manor House at Kelmscott with his wife Janey and the poet and painter Rossetti. Undeterred by his friend's justifiable complaints about the unhealthy air of this low-lying village, Morris used it as a base for enthusiastic exploration of the Cotswold countryside. (For a time he stayed in the spectacularly sited Broadway Tower, but Rossetti objected to the climb.) In the traditional methods of Cotswold craftsmen and builders Morris found confirmation of his socialist belief in the ennoblement of man liberated by handicraft from the curse of the machine. Inspired by his enthusiasm, several of his disciples moved into the Cotswolds: Ernest Gimson, the furniture maker, Edward and Sidney Barnsley, and Norman Jewson, who all worked on Rodmarton Manor. Lord Bathurst encouraged them and lent them Pinbury Park, north of Sapperton, for their workshops. (Arlington Mill Museum has an excellent display of their work.) In 1901 C.R. Ashbee moved the 50 members of his Guild of Handicrafts (founded 1888) and their families from the East End of London to Chipping Campden, revitalising this somnolent town. Few of them responded to Ashbee's idea that they should support themselves by tilling the land as well as pursuing their crafts after the Guild went bankrupt in 1905. The hand-made products were too expensive for most people, but they awakened interest in Cotswold traditional crafts and attracted visitors, who were already being drawn by popularising accounts and paintings of the picturesque scenery. By 1930 tourism had become crucial to the Cotswold economy.

To some extent the increased understanding of Cotswold crafts and traditions has been fruitless, because traditional methods and materials are now too

► *A stretch of the disused Thames and Severn Canal (opened 1789) in Coates parish, an elaborate feat of engineering in its day but never a financial success; the Oxford Canal took its trade and its water soaked away through the porous limestone. It was closed in 1933 and is now secluded and overgrown*

▼ *Old cloth mills in the Golden Valley near Stroud, which is dotted with these relics of the Cotswolds' most important industry. Some date back to the 17th century; most were extended and rebuilt in the brief early-19th-century cloth boom, and many have now been converted to other industrial uses*

costly for any but the very wealthy. The modern artificial substitute for Cotswold stone, made of crushed limestone, does not weather quite so attractively as real stone. But planners respect the importance of the Cotswold vernacular style to the beauty of the landscape, and stringent restrictions on new building impose conformity to long-established patterns and a sensitive blend of old and new, safeguarding the distinctiveness of the Cotswold scene.

The modern Cotswolds are generally prosperous, although, as in all rural areas, mechanisation of agriculture has drastically reduced the number of jobs available, so that most people in the villages have to commute to the towns to earn their living. Many have gone altogether, to be replaced by holiday or retirement home-owners, who bring money to the area but live there only part-time. Reproducing a pattern common to other regions of outstanding natural beauty, they raise property prices beyond the reach of the local population and fragment the sense of community, even whilst assiduously preserving and restoring the Cotswold architecture and landscape. There are fewer village inns and shops than there were before the war, despite the annual influx of tourists, who tend to cluster about the well-known resorts – Bourton-on-the-Water, Broadway, Burford and Chipping Campden. All these places are in the north or east Cotswolds, an easy distance from Birmingham, Coventry, Oxford or Cheltenham: until recently the southern parts, more remote from major cities, were far less visited and appreciated. The M4 motorway has made a radical difference. The physical change was dramatic: the huge amounts of gravel needed for its construction were excavated from pits around South Cerney, which were then filled with water and converted into the Cotswold Water Park, a prime attraction for sportsmen and naturalists. The economic change was even greater: the south Cotswolds were now within easy reach of

*Two contrasting views of the Cotswolds, illustrating their secret and open aspects:* below, Stanton vicarage, half hidden at the end of a long drive, the sun filtering through the foliage bringing a glow to the golden stone; right, Naunton, spread out along the Windrush valley and flanked by exhilarating open country, a chequerboard of ploughland and pasture. In the foreground is a good example of a traditional Cotswold dry stone wall

London and attracted numerous immigrants, amongst them several members of the royal family – the Prince and Princess of Wales at Highgrove House, near Tetbury; Princess Anne and Captain Mark Phillips 6 miles away at Gatcombe Park; and Prince and Princess Michael of Kent at Nether Lypiatt Manor, near Stroud.

The rural Cotswolds have always been feudal and they remain so, in economic fact if not in social practice. Great estates are still bought by private citizens (Salperton changed hands for £3,000,000 in 1981), though now more often by wealthy business families, such as the Vesteys at Stowell, than by the landed gentry. The aristocracy continues to exert power and influence: Lord Bathurst's estate still runs from the centre of Cirencester to Sapperton, almost 5 miles to the west. The royal immigrants have settled near 'Beaufortshire', that area around Badminton owned by their friend, the benevolently paternalistic 10th Duke of Beaufort, who is reputed to know every blade of grass on his estate. But at the same time the Cotswolds have accommodated to the 20th century, and alongside this landed wealth modern technology contributes to the region's prosperity. Prospecting for oil has begun; Fairford, famous for the 15th-century stained glass of its church, is now as well known for Concorde, based at an airstrip nearby; and at Postlip, in an Anglo-Saxon mill, a firm which has made paper since the 18th century produces glass-fibre-loaded filter paper, used to prevent the escape of radioactive particles from nuclear power stations.

# Places of interest in the Cotswolds: a gazetteer

*The reference after each place-name is to the map at the end of the book*

**Ablington** (D4)  Tiny village on the R. Coln. Imposing houses with luxuriant gardens glimpsed behind high walls and hedges. Manor House (1590) opposite two huge barns. Ablington House (*c*1650) has stone lions from the Houses of Parliament on its gateposts.

**Adlestrop** (F6)  Adlestrop Park, originally a monastic barn, was converted into a house (late 17th century) and remodelled in gothick style by Sanderson Miller (1750–62); he also altered the over-restored church. 18th-century cottages in the village. In 1806 Jane Austen stayed at the Old Rectory, now Adlestrop House, with her relation Thomas Leigh, owner of Stoneleigh Abbey, Warwickshire. She later described him as 'the possessor of one of the finest Estates in England & of more worthless Nephews and Neices than any other private Man in the United Kingdoms'. 'Adlestrop', Edward Thomas' most famous poem, was inspired by an unexpected stop at the railway station, now closed (its name-plate has been moved to the bus shelter).

**Aldsworth** (E5)  Upland village which prospered when Bibury race-course was in use, hence its solid late-18th- and early-19th-century cottages. The church, w of the scrubby village green, has an octagonal spire, bold carvings of grotesque heads and animals on the n aisle exterior (*c*1500) above lavishly ornamental window surrounds, and a rib-vaulted n porch with a niche to hold candles (perhaps a chantry).

**Ampney Crucis** (D4)  The church stands below the wall of Ampney Park, a 16th-century manor house with additions from every succeeding century. Saxon doorway in nave n wall. Late Norman chancel arch. Remnants of 14th-century wall-painting in n transept. Crumbling monument to George Lloyd and his wife (1584), shown lying beneath a canopy supported by columns, all carved in rich detail from exquisite pale freestone. Memorials to the Pleydell family of Ampney Park (1561–1724) record the hours as well as the dates of their deaths. The early-15th-century head of the churchyard cross was discovered walled up in the rood loft in 1860.

**Ampney St Mary** (D4)  The church stands in fields by the A417 apart from the village, now to the NE at Ashbrook. Early-12th-century nave. Carved lintel over n doorway, showing a griffon and a lion which tramples two snakes with sinister faces (their bodies form the roll-moulding below the lintel), perhaps symbolising the triumph of good over evil. Several fine tombs in the churchyard. Interior with superb timber waggon roofs and stone screen (a rare survival). Beautiful w window with flowing tracery in the Decorated style, unusual in the Cotswolds. Extensive fragmentary wall-paintings (12th–15th centuries); that on the s wall, of Christ injured by manual labour on Sundays, includes details of medieval crafts, e.g. a wheelwright truing a spoke by holding it to his eye.

**Ampney St Peter** (D4)  Church restored by Giles Gilbert Scott, 1898. Saxon

*◄ Bibury church: the tall chancel arch was built in the 13th century onto Saxon jambs and sculpted imposts, and probably at the same time the chancel was lengthened and given its three imposing lancet windows. In summer the church affords a peaceful retreat from the much-visited village*

nave and tower arch. Ancient fertility carving, N of the 15th-century font. 14th-century churchyard cross.

**Arlington** see **Bibury**

**Avening** (B3) Site of a pagan Saxon cemetery. Church with early Norman central tower, nave, N aisle, chancel arch and rib vault in the chancel's first bay (extended in the 14th century, when the timber nave roof was constructed). 17th-century monuments include, in the N transept, the kneeling effigy of Henry Brydges (1615), son of Lord Chandos of Sudeley. Having been a notorious pirate, he married a wealthy clothier's daughter and settled down at Avening Court to lead a blameless life. Three Neolithic burial chambers on a hillside ¼ mile N of the church include England's only accessible example of a porthole entrance. The Tingle Stone in Gatcombe Park, N of the village, runs round its field when it hears the church clock strike midnight. Gatcombe Park mansion, 1771–4 with extensions by Basevi (who also worked on Painswick House), was built for a descendant of the pirate Brydges' father-in-law, Edward Sheppard, also a clothier; it is now the home of Princess Anne and Captain Mark Phillips.

**Badminton** (B2: two villages, Great and Little Badminton) At Great Badminton estate cottages surround the large village green, which includes a cricket pitch. 18th-century terraces and almshouses line the road to the entrance gates of Badminton House, the earliest and greatest classical mansion of the Cotswolds, begun after the Restoration by Henry Somerset, 1st Duke of Beaufort (open to the public on Wednesday afternoons in summer). The hall, part of the first stage of building, determined the size of the badminton court – the game was first played here. Sumptuous interiors, with a good collection of pictures, and Grinling Gibbons carvings in the dining room. House enlarged and park remodelled by William Kent (1746). His Worcester Lodge on the

▲ *Badminton: the church (1785) is attached to the Duke of Beaufort's mansion, epitomising the 18th-century Anglican Tory establishment. It contains several grand family monuments*

Didmarton road, a beautiful big Palladian gateway, formerly a summerhouse (the upper storey is a dining room), closes the 3-mile vista from the N door. The Beaufort Hunt is one of the great traditionally English institutions of the Cotswolds; the 5th duke, who is said to have invented fox hunting after a disappointing pursuit of deer, popularised the sport in the mid 18th century. Badminton Horse Trials, equally famous, were instituted by the 10th duke in 1949 and are held in the park every spring.

Great Badminton church (1785), replacing a medieval one demolished by the 5th duke, is connected to the mansion by a corridor from the library to 'the tribune' – the Somerset family pew, a gallery at the back of the church containing a fireplace and comfortable armchairs. Splendid series of ducal monuments, notably by Rysbrack, to the 2nd and 3rd dukes (E end of the aisle). The gigantic memorial in the chancel to the 1st duke by Grinling Gibbons, whose genius for carving wood did not extend to stone, was originally in St George's Chapel, Windsor; Queen Victoria had to pay for Badminton's chancel to get rid of it.

Little Badminton, less emphatically in the Beaufort demesne, has a circular and gabled dovecote on its village green.

**Bagendon** (C4) Capital of the Cotswolds under the Dubonni (1st century), now a tiny village. Their settlement occupied several hundred acres, bounded by a steep slope and a great system of defensive dykes (sections are still visible along the Woodmancote–Perrott's Brook road, now covered by beechwood). Excavation revealed traces of a mint and houses of the traditional circular plan. Imported goods, e.g. Italian wine jars and Egyptian glass, now in the Corinium

▼ *Bourton-on-the-Water in spring: the River Windrush, spanned by low footbridges, runs alongside the main street. In summer it can scarcely be seen through the crowds of visitors to this famously picturesque village*

Museum, Cirencester, indicate prosperity, but after the Romans founded Corinium Bagendon declined. The church, shaded by a fine variety of evergreens, has some Norman architecture – the lower stages of the pretty saddlebacked tower and the late N arcade of the nave. Trinity Mill, recorded in the Domesday Book, is pre-Conquest.

**Barnsley** (D4)  Harmonious estate village on the A33. Church with Norman N doorway, piers of chancel arch and grotesque heads on chancel exterior. Rebuilding in the 15th century (financed by Sir Edmund Tame of Fairford) and the 19th; the odd top stage of the tower, with four domestic-looking gables, was completed c1600. Cottages mostly 17th and 19th century. Barnsley Park, N of the village (viewing by appointment), is an 18th-century baroque mansion partly remodelled by Nash, built of beautiful and very well preserved stone. Sumptuous plasterwork in the entrance hall. Barnsley House, s of the village, is an attractive and substantial 17th-century dwelling.

**Barton** see **Temple Guiting**

**Batsford** (E7)  First recorded in the 8th century as part of a sheep-rearing estate given by King Ethelbald of Mercia to the Bishop of Worcester, who later lost it to a greedy nobleman of Ethelred the Unready. Acquired in the 18th century by the 1st Baron Redesdale (ancestor of the Mitford sisters). Handsome church (rebuilt 1861–2) by the driveway to Batsford Park, an 'Elizabethan' mansion with arts-and-crafts ornament designed by Ernest George for a later Baron Redesdale in 1888. Famous garden (open to the public) with a large collection of trees, shrubs, Chinese temples and buddhas.

**Baunton** (D4)  Norman church, notable for its brightly coloured 14th-century

►*Burford church. The earliest part is the Norman base of the tower; the spire and bell stage are 15th century. Standing at the north end of the town beside the River Windrush, the church is a prominent landmark and elegantly closes the view down the High Street. This picture shows (left to right) the south transept, chapel of the Holy Trinity, and chancel – of various dates but with windows mostly of the 15th century, when the church was extensively remodelled by local wool merchants*

▼ *Broadway: 18th-century Picton House, a fine example of the many handsome old houses lining the main street of this exceptionally beautiful village*

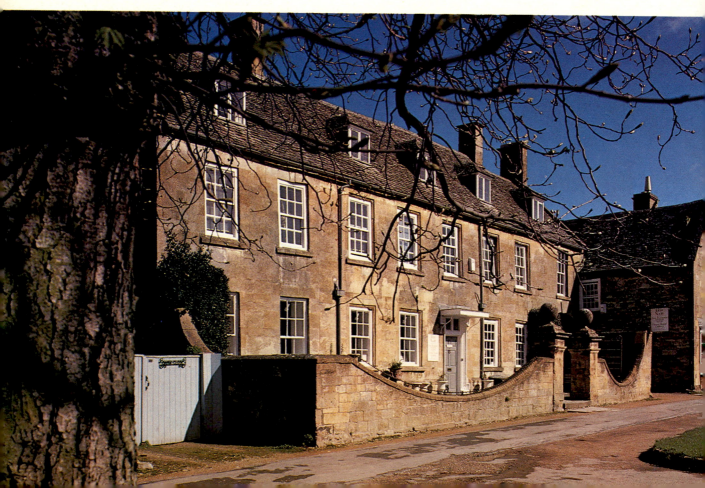

wall-painting of St Christopher, in a red cloak, carrying the Christ-child across a river which bears two ships and a mermaid with her mirror. On the right is a hermit with a lantern by a church; on the left, a seated figure fishing. On the s wall, behind a curtain, a 15th-century embroidered silk altar frontal (a very rare survival) depicts the Crucifixion and, below, a rebus of an eagle grasping an ass above a barrel sprouting branches – a visual pun which has not yet been satisfactorily explained.

**Belas Knap** (C6)  The best-preserved long barrow (megalithic burial chamber) in England, constructed *c*3000 BC on the edge above Winchcombe near Humblebee Wood (OS SP 021254), and isolated amidst barley fields. The name probably derives from Anglo-Saxon *bel*, 'beacon', and *cnaepp*, 'hill-top'. A signposted path up the hill affords splendid views of Sudeley and Winchcombe and N to the Vale of Evesham and W to the Malverns. The mound, bordered by a dry stone wall, is max. 54 m long and 4 m high and covered with wild thyme, rockrose and scabious. It was badly excavated 1863–5, revealing three entrances to burial chambers containing numerous skeletons. At the N end a false entrance between two horns encloses a U-shaped forecourt, probably of ritual significance. In 1931 local men rebuilt part of the wall, using the same skills as their predecessors 5000 years before.

**Beverston** (B3)  Beverston Castle (not open to the public but clearly visible from the church) is a substantial ruin incorporating a still-inhabited early-17th-century house on the site of its s range. The earliest parts, a quadrangle with drum towers at each corner, date from *c*1225. Lord Berkeley, who bought the manor in 1330, added the W range, chapel and gatehouse. During the Civil War an amateur garrison put up a successful defence against Parliamentarian forces until its leader, Colonel Ogilthorpe, was captured during a nocturnal assignation with a girl from Chavenage House. Church with Saxon sculpture of the Resurrection on the tower's s face, late Norman s doorway decorated with art nouveau-like leaf pattern and very fine early-13th-century s nave arcade. An attractive priest's door in the chancel looks Regency gothick but is actually 14th century. Complicated roof (1844) by Louis Vulliamy, who also designed many cottages in the village.

**Bibury** (D4)  One of the Cotswolds' prettiest and most visited villages. Houses and manor (17th-century Bibury Court, now a hotel) cluster round the tall spacious church set in a graveyard full of table tombs and roses. The Abbey of Osney near Oxford appropriated the original minster church (1151) and greatly enlarged it, adding the nave arcades. Especially grand N arcade, with finely carved capitals. Square font, very late Norman. 17th-century Bibury was famous for horse racing; in 1681, when Parliament met at Oxford, Charles II transferred the Newmarket spring meeting here and started a series of events lasting into the 19th century. Horses and stables remain very evident in the village.

Arlington Mill, probably 17th century, between Bibury and the hamlet of Arlington, is now a museum. Working machinery from North Cerney mill. Interesting display of furniture by Ernest Gimson, C.R. Ashbee and Sidney Barnsley, leaders of the Cotswold arts and crafts movement. The mill stream is now a fish farm: fat trout fill the R. Coln, alongside the road. Creeper-covered Swan Hotel has a beautiful shellhood doorway. Picturesque Arlington Row, the most famous group of cottages in the Cotswolds, was converted from a monastic wool barn into weavers' homes in the 17th century. It faces Rack Isle, a 4-acre

*▲ Burford in stormy weather. Attractive houses of varied periods and styles line the High Street, which slopes down to the Windrush. The 16th-century Corner House Hotel, one of the most decorative of the many historic inns built to cater for Burford's coach trade, retains the original wooden-framed mullioned windows of its timber-framed upper storey*

water meadow where cloth was hung to dry before being fulled at the mill, and now a National Trust preserve for water fowl. Attractive cottages up the hill around Arlington village green.

**Birdlip** (C5)  In beechwoods on a sharp bend in the A417. Iron Age burial site: the Birdlip Mirror, a superb example of Celtic workmanship, was unearthed here (now in Gloucester City Museum). 19th-century inns recall Birdlip's past as a regular coach-halt, their extensive stables now mostly replaced by farm buildings.

**Bisley** (B4)  Large grey stone village. Church (mostly 13th and 14th centuries, much restored in the 1800s) on a hill of pre-Christian sanctity. Roman altars, discovered during restoration, were probably associated with the wells fed by seven springs below the hill. Every Ascension Day local children decorate the wells with flowers – a custom thought up in 1863 by Thomas Keble, John's younger brother. Churchyard (affording good views of fine 17th- and 18th-century wool merchants' houses) with lantern-like structure where candles were placed for masses for the poor – the only outside example in England, said to commemorate a priest who drowned in a well one night on his way to a dying parishioner. Bear Inn, formerly the court house. Lock-up with two cells dated 1824 in George Street. Jayne's Court (early 18th century), sw of the church, has an octagonal dovecote and a cockpit. Wesley House, Church Hill, is a reminder that Wesley preached here.

Lypiatt, one of several hamlets hidden in surrounding valleys, has three manors: Tudor Middle Lypiatt; late-14th-century Lypiatt Park at Upper Lypiatt (enlarged 1809 by Wyatville); and Nether Lypiatt, exquisitely early

31

18th century, grand in conception but doll's-house in scale, set back from the road behind delicate wrought-iron gates. Now owned by Prince and Princess Michael of Kent, it is locally said to be one of the most haunted houses in the area.

**Blockley** (E7) became the Bishop of Worcester's property in 1002 and remained part of Worcestershire until 1931. Late Norman church, faced with golden ashlar. 18th-century gothick spire with a classical window. Excellent N aisle monuments, mostly 16th–19th-century memorials to the Rushout family who built nearby Northwick Park (1686, remodelled 1730 by Lord Burlington; not open to the public). Note especially the monument to Anne Mary Childe (1659), which shows her reclining in front of a bookcase; the books have their spines to the wall, in 17th-century fashion. Pretty Regency terraces, some with wrought-iron porches, built for workers at the six (now defunct) silk mills. The mainly 17th–18th-century Manor House, S of the church, is probably on the site of the Bishop of Worcester's summer residence.

**Bourton-on-the-Hill** (F7) Church and village of orange stone. Attractive buildings in the long steep main street (A44) include a Retreat for the Aged (1831) and the 18th-century Horse and Groom Inn. Massive barn dated 1570 amongst outbuildings of Bourton House (18th century) at E end of village.

**Bourton-on-the-Water** (E6) Exceptionally pretty village on the R. Windrush, a Roman settlement with Iron Age origins. Visitors are attracted by Birdland (a famous collection of rare and exotic birds), the model village (a scale replica of Bourton which includes a model of the model), and the old water mill housing a motor museum. The church, an astonishing medley, has an 18th-century tower, medieval chancel overwhelmed inside by a modern painted roof, and Victorian nave designed by Sir Thomas Jackson, which is handsomely proportioned but blighted by effete stained glass.

*Chipping Campden from a distance* (below) *is dominated by the tall 15th-century tower of its magnificent wool church; beyond is the edge of the scarp slope, the Cotswolds' western boundary.* Right, *part of the High Street showing* (left) *The Martins, an early-18th-century house near the market hall — an especially delightful example of the rich variety of architecture in the Cotswolds' most attractive market town*

**Broadway** (D7) Probably the most visited village in the Cotswolds. The spacious long High Street, leading to the steep ascent of Fish Hill, has houses and inns of every period, most of golden Guiting stone, set behind wide grass verges. The earliest include Lygon Arms, once the manor house, dated 1620 but with some early-16th-century portions, Tudor House (1660) and 18th-century Broad Close and Picton House, all impressive. Gordon Russell's well-known furniture factory began by making furniture for the Lygon Arms; its High Street frontage is partly 16th century, partly Georgian. Abbot's Grange (at the end of Church Street near the green), 14th century with Elizabethan alterations, was the Abbot of Evesham's summer house. St Eadburga's, the original parish church, basically Norman with a 15th-century exterior, lies beautiful and unspoilt 1 mile s amid varied trees and rolling fields. Fine 14th-century tower arches and timber nave roof. Its elaborate Elizabethan pulpit is now in St Michael's, Church Street (1839). Broadway Tower (SE), 305 m above sea level, a folly built for the Earl of Coventry in 1800, affords spectacular views across the Vale of Evesham to Bredon Hill and beyond to the Malverns. Middle Hill House to the s (1725) belonged in the early 1800s to the bibliomaniac Sir Thomas Phillipps, who said 'I wish to have one copy of every Book in the World'. Sales of his books and MSS at intervals since his death have not yet exhausted his collection. His first wife was driven to the bottle and his second to a distant spa; he forbade his eldest daughter's marriage, locking up her clothes to prevent her leaving, but she eloped, cheered on her way by the whole village.

**Buckland** (D7) Famous for its 15th-century rectory, the oldest in Gloucestershire still used as such (occasionally open to the public). Imposing hall with fine open timber roof and 15th-century stained glass showing the courtship dance ('leck') of the blackcock – a display so elaborate that blackcock were suspected

◄ *Chipping Campden church: the wall monument to Penelope Noel in the Earl of Gainsborough's mortuary chapel. She died young in 1633 from blood poisoning, caused by pricking her finger whilst doing embroidery*

of being witches in disguise, and so fiercely suppressed that they disappeared from some counties. However these blackcock dispel the suspicion by carrying in their beaks scrolls saying 'In nomine Jesu'. Partly 13th-century church with 15th-century tiles, stained glass and benches and 17th- and 18th-century seating and wainscotting (including hat-pegs). Its greatest treasure, the 16th-century Buckland bowl, formerly used as a loving-cup at village weddings, is of maple with a silver rim and a disc in the centre showing St Margaret trampling the dragon.

**Burford** (F5) One of the Cotswolds' finest market towns (charter granted 1087). The impressively wide High Street runs downhill to a medieval pack-horse bridge spanning the Windrush. Many substantial houses erected with fortunes made in the wool trade, e.g. Falkland Hall (1588) on the corner of Priory Lane, built one of Burford's greatest clothier families, the Sylvesters. After the market declined in the 17th century the coach trade remained important until the 19th, hence the numerous inns, the George (late 15th century) and the Bull (16th century with a jolly 18th-century front) being amongst the oldest. The church, originally Norman as the central tower and w wall of the nave show, was totally remodelled in the 15th century with wool trade money. s porch and spire c1450. The Lady Chapel (built c1200 by the Guild of Merchants), originally separate from the main church, was joined to it in the late 15th century, creating an interior of almost cathedral-like spaciousness. Restorers in the 1870s stripped the interior walls of their medieval plaster, so enraging William Morris that he founded the Society for the Protection of Ancient Buildings. He was right – unplastered rubble walls, especially on this scale, are exceptionally ugly; but Burford's vicar said 'The church, Sir, is mine, and if I choose to I shall stand on my head in it.' Several Lady Chapel tombs belonging to guildsmen bear merchants' marks. In the N aisle a monument to Edward Harman, one of Henry VIII's barber surgeons, features Red Indians. St Catherine's Chapel, N of the chancel, is dominated by the sumptuous monument of Sir Lawrence Tanfield and his wife (1628). Church Lane has 15th-century almshouses founded by Warwick the Kingmaker, and on the corner the old grammar school (16th century), where the poet John Wilmot, Earl of Rochester, was educated. The bustle of the High Street contrasts with the serenity of Sheep Street, at right angles to it, where formerly the sheep market was held.

**Cassey Compton** see **Withington**

**Chalford** (B4) Large industrial village on a hillside terraced for mills, weavers' cottages, clothiers' fine houses and fields for racks to dry the cloth. Many of its streets are too steep and narrow for cars. The Company's Arms, 15th century with an early-18th-century façade, originally the manor house, became an inn for visiting merchants. Refugee Huguenot weavers occupied Grey Cot in the 17th century. St Mary's Mill House, begun c1710, stands by its owner's mill (c1820), which now makes walking sticks. The Thames and Severn Canal runs through Chalford; the round lengthsman's house is a canal museum.

**Chavenage** (B3) E-shaped manor house (1576, incorporating parts of an earlier building) erected for Edward Stephens, whose initials are carved beside the front doorway, probably using stone from Horsley Priory ruins nearby. Imposing hall with two tall windows and elaborate 17th-century chimney-piece. The Oak Room has partly gilded panelling (1627) and fine views across trim lawns to the Marlborough Downs. In 1648 Cromwell and Ireton visited

Chavenage to persuade its owner, Colonel Nathaniel Stephens, to vote for Charles I's impeachment. He reluctantly agreed and his daughter cursed him as a regicide; soon afterwards he fell ill, but left his bed to enter a mysterious dark coach that drew up outside. Onlookers had time to notice that the driver was headless and dressed in royal robes before the coach disappeared in flames. Cromwell's Room in the SE wing is fitted with Mortlake tapestry. The present chapel (*c*1800) replaces one that was begun as a folly in the early 18th century. Saxon font, discovered in the foundations of a barn on the estate. Superb carved 16th-century altar frontal, perhaps originally an over-mantel in the house, which contains much excellent 16th- and 17th-century furniture. (Open two afternoons a week in summer.)

**Chedworth** (D5) One of the country's best-preserved Roman villas, *c*180–*c*350 AD, in a beautiful woodland setting in the Coln valley; discovered (1864) by a rabbiting party digging for a lost ferret, and now a National Trust property with a small museum. Mosaic floors, excellently preserved hypocaust (under-floor heating system), and remains of two bath suites. Chedworth village has a late Norman church with a 15th-century s façade, said to have been financed by the Duke of Clarence (who owned the manor), and a tall elegant 15th-century pulpit.

**Chipping Campden** (E8) The most beautiful and best-preserved Cotswold market town, historic centre of the area's wool trade ('Chipping' derives from Anglo-Saxon *ceapen*, 'market'). Graceful curving main street, its picturesque-

► *The impressive interior of Cirencester parish church, seen from the north aisle and looking east towards (left to right) the Lady Chapel, the Chapel of St Catherine and the chancel. The lofty nave piers were erected 1516–30. The painted stone pulpit is 15th century; its open tracery is unique*

▼ *Cirencester churchyard, a quiet refuge from the busy market on the other side of a row of houses. The tower, begun c1400, was intended to have a spire, but this was found to be structurally impossible*

ness increased by wide verges and trees. There was a weekly market here by 1200; wool made the fortunes of several townsmen, notably William Grevel, ancestor of the earls of Warwick, who built himself Grevel House (late 14th century) in the High Street, and Sir Baptist Hicks, donor of the almshouses near the church (1612). The gateway next to the church between two imposing lodges and the two pavilions in the field behind are the only remnants of Sir Baptist's great mansion, burnt down in the Civil War. Other notable buildings include Woolstaplers Hall (High Street, late 14th century), beautiful 18th-century Dover's House, and the Regency Cotswold House Hotel with an elegant circular staircase under a dome.

The church, originally Norman, was transformed in the 15th century with wool merchants' money into one of the grandest and most harmonious of Cotswold buildings. The spacious nave (c1488), flooded with light from its great windows and clerestory, has octagonal piers with concave surfaces, looking oddly eastern – presumably designed by the same mason as the very similar ones at Northleach. The large window over the chancel arch, a Cotswold characteristic, has stained glass almost as ugly as the E window's grey-faced figures in a rock garden. Pulpit (1612) and late-15th-century eagle lectern given by Sir Baptist Hicks. In cases below the tower are superb 15th-century altar hangings which show why English embroidery was esteemed the best in Europe during the Middle Ages. Fine monuments in the Earl of Gainsborough's mortuary chapel: to Sir Baptist Hicks and his wife (1629), perhaps by Nicholas Stone – large and ornate but not overpowering, being made entirely of

*Cirencester's varied architecture:* left, *the Old House in Gloucester Street, early 18th century with a Regency wing, was once a mill and tannery;* below, *the surviving part of St John's Hospital in Spitalgate, founded by Henry I – four bays of the hall arcade*

chaste grey and white stone exquisitely carved, especially in the details of costume; and to Edward Noel, Viscount Campden, and Juliana his wife (1664), poised in their shrouds at the open door of their tomb.

**Cirencester** (D4, and see street plan above) Under Diocletian, as capital of one of four Roman British sub-provinces, Corinium enclosed 240 acres, second only to London in size, and as Cirencester it is still the largest town in the Cotswolds. Corinium Museum, Park Street, houses Roman remains. A basilica and baths have been located. The amphitheatre outside the town walls is now the 'Bull Ring', a grassy hollow. Medieval Cirencester was the centre of the Cotswolds' wool trade. The abbey (founded 1107 by Henry I) dominated the town with lasting effect: Cirencester is not a borough and has no mayor because the abbots successfully defeated all attempts to secure a charter of incorporation. At the Reformation Robert Basinge bought the abbey and scrupulously obeyed instructions to leave not a single stone on top of another: only 'Saxon Arch' in Grove Lane, the abbey's (Norman) gatehouse, survives.

The church of St John the Baptist, the largest parish church in Gloucestershire, dominates the market place. Its tower was rebuilt with the usurping Henry IV's reward to the townspeople for capturing and executing the Earls of Salisbury and Kent, Richard II's half-brothers (1400). Further rebuilding (15th and early 16th centuries) by Cirencester's woolmen and weavers, notably the Garstang, Dixton and Prelatte families. The elaborate three-storied fan-vaulted s porch (1490), erected as offices by the abbot, served for centuries after the Dissolution as the town hall. Nave rebuilt and clerestory added 1521, creating a spacious interior. Carved angels above the nave's piers carry shields bearing the arms or merchants' marks of men who financed the rebuilding. St Catherine's Chapel, beautifully fan-vaulted (1508), has 15th-century wall-paintings of St Catherine and St Christopher. In the Lady Chapel (rebuilt 1450) the large early-17th-century monument to Humfry Bridges and his wife also shows their 11 children.

As excellent views from the church tower make clear, one of Cirencester's most pleasing features is the proximity of open land to the bustling centre – the abbey grounds (N), the churchyard (E), and Cirencester Park (W), where an immensely tall semicircular yew hedge (gardeners need a fireman's crane to clip the top) conceals the mansion built 1714–18 by Allen Apsley, 1st Lord Bathurst, and still owned by his family. His friend Alexander Pope advised him in laying out the park (open to the public), a massive operation. Ten rides segment it, radiating from the midpoint of Broad Avenue, which runs straight through the whole estate from the mansion to Sapperton nearly 5 miles W – the finest example of formal park planning in the country, and untouched by the fashion for 'natural' landscaping in the next generation because Lord Bathurst lived to an advanced age. However, the artificial lake and occasional serpentine walk add a note of studied picturesqueness, as does Alfred's Hall (1721–32), the first castellated folly in England. Lord Bathurst himself designed the Hexagon (1736). 'Pope's Seat' is a small rusticated pavilion. Famous beech plantations attract foresters from all over the world. But Pope commented: 'Join Cotswold Hills to Sapperton's fair dale . . . Link towns to towns with avenues of oak,/ Enclose whole downs in walls, 'tis all a joke!/Inexorable Death shall level all,/ And trees, and stones, and farms, and farmer fall.'

Fine 17th- and 18th-century wool merchants' houses include Park House (1725), Dollar Street, and Abberley House, Park Street. Narrow curved Cox-

▶ *Daglingworth: the Crucifixion, one of four pieces of late Saxon sculpture for which the church is famous. The soldiers bear (left) the spear and scourge and (right) the reed and sponge. This piece was found during restoration work (1845–50) built into the chancel arch*

well Street, virtually unchanged for three centuries, is lined with rubble-built gabled houses, some enclosing attractive little alleys and courtyards. Cecily Hill, a wide avenue leading into the Park, has several handsome houses and extraordinary embattled Barracks (1857).

**Coates** (C4) Pleasing group of Norman church with beautiful 15th-century w tower, Church Farm (17th century, formerly the manor house), and early-19th-century Old Rectory. Gargoyle on sw corner of the church tower of a cannibal having his dinner. Cottages and houses designed by Barnsley and Jewson. One of the five roundhouses built *c*1789 for Thames and Severn Canal lengthsmen is at Coates.

**Coberley** (C5) Access to the church through an arch in farm buildings. 15th-century tower adorned with gargoyles, arms of the Berkeleys of Coberley and (on the s) a sundial (1693). s doorway and chapel built *c*1340 by Sir Thomas Berkeley. Hoodmoulds on the exterior of two chapel windows have finely carved headstops, one of a young man with exquisitely detailed hair. Detailed carving also of acorns and foliage on the capitals of the nave and chancel, handsomely rebuilt 1869–72. The chancel contains the heart-burial monument of Sir Giles Berkeley (1295), a small bust of a knight in chainmail. His charger, Lombard, is buried in the churchyard, on the other side of the wall. Large mid-14th-century effigies in s chapel of Sir Thomas Berkeley, who fought at Crécy, and his wife Joan, the mother of Dick Whittington by her next husband. The small effigy beside them, a girl holding a glove, probably portrays one of their daughters. A recess in the s wall contains an effigy of a young man in 14th-century dress, again with finely carved long curled hair. High walls on the

► *Ebrington church: the Norman nave, looking west. The south aisle and chancel arch are 13th century, the font 15th century; the pulpit is carved with the date 1679. The spacious barn-like interior is typical of many Cotswold village churches*

▼ *Donnington: Arkell's Brewery (the only one in the Cotswolds), a family firm established in 1865. Donnington ales are sold in 17 inns, none more than 15 miles from the brewery*

◄ *Duntisbourne Rouse: the partly Saxon church stands on a steep slope, which enabled a crypt to be constructed under the chancel – an unusual feature in a village church. The saddle-backed (gabled) tower was completed in 1587. The contrast between the lush and beautiful scenery and the austere, almost grim, architecture of an ancient church is to be found in several Cotswold villages*

E and s sides of the churchyard with two 17th-century doorways are remains of the manor house, demolished in the 18th century.

**Cold Ashton** (A1)  Southernmost tip of the Cotswolds. Manor house gables peer over high walls. Church rebuilt 1508–40 (except for 14th-century tower) by the rector, Thomas Key – his rebus, a T and a key, appears on the window mouldings. Oak pulpit with elaborately crocketed stone canopy of great beauty.

**Coln Rogers** (D4)  Named after Roger of Gloucester, who in 1150 gave it to the monks of Gloucester. Church with complete Saxon nave. The monks inserted the s doorway and lengthened the chancel. Medieval oak chest with its original ironwork. Fireplace in the nave's N wall.

**Coln St Aldwyns** (E4)  The descent from Hatherop gives a pleasing view of the village in its valley, set on the edge of beautiful parkland. Church with Norman s doorway and, to its E, carving over a blocked Norman window of a demon biting a man's hand. 16th-century manor house with square dovecote. Attractive 17th-century houses around the village green.

**Coln St Dennis** (D5)  Well-preserved Norman church. Splendidly humpy central tower, whose NE buttress seems to reach down to clutch the nave. Norman grotesque heads of beaked or grimacing animals have been reused as corbels for the nave roof. Norman tower arch, Early English chancel arch on Norman shafts and capitals. The half-door of the N porch produces a rather stable-like effect; graffiti carved on it include the date 1637.

**Condicote** (E6)  One of the loneliest and most ancient villages on the wolds, on Ryknield Street, a route that was old when the Romans took it over. Bronze Age circular earthwork enclosure E of the village. Circular village green surrounded by a dry stone wall. 14th-century wayside cross. 12th-century church: narrow richly ornamented s doorway with diapered tympanum with carved shafts. Excellent views on the road to Hinchwick Manor, 1 mile N, designed 1826 by C.R. Cockerell (gardens occasionally open to the public).

**Cotswold Farm Park** (E6),  2 miles E of Guiting Power. In 1970 25 acres of rough upland pasture on Bemborough Farm, their surface pitted by the quarry-ing of stone for roof tiles, were converted into a conservation centre for rare breeds of farm animals (open to the public). Fascinating specimens of animals common in medieval or more recent times but rare today include the Bagot goat, first imported from Switzerland by Richard I; the four-horned Viking Manx Loghtan sheep; Gloucester Old Spot pigs, once owned by every cottager in the Cotswolds; Old Gloucester cows, England's rarest cattle, from whose milk Double Gloucester cheese was first made; and the Cotswold sheep, the origin of the area's prosperity.

**Cranham** (B5)  Village at the head of the Painswick valley amid woods of great botanical richness. Heavily restored 15th-century church with sheep shears carved on its tower. Iron Age hill fort ½ mile NW, typical of the many dotted along the scarp slope.

**Cricklade** (E3)  Small town on the Cotswolds' SE border, first important as a strongpoint in King Alfred's defences against the Danes. Church of St Samson (died *c*565), a Celtic saint and missionary in Cornwall and Britanny supposedly buried below an earthwork at Cairn Hill, SW of Malmesbury. Distinctively Wiltshire massive 16th-century tower with large corner pinnacles. Interior darkened by modern stained glass in a variety of styles, all repellent and depressing. Refreshing sense of air and light below the tower, which has a splendid lierne vault with richly carved bosses, its lofty arches decorated with prominent carved coats of arms. St Mary's church, on the N side of the town, has a squat tower, dormer windows in the nave roof, a Norman chancel arch and box pews. Well-preserved medieval churchyard cross with canopied figures supported by four angels carrying shields.

**Daglingworth** (C4) Church noted for its Saxon features. Saxon narrow S doorway and sundial above it. 15th-century S door. Small Saxon crucifix by the pulpit, originally on the outer E wall. Roman inscribed stone panel with two lancet windows cut into it, originally at the E end of the Saxon chancel, in the N vestry wall. Three Saxon sculptures, found in the chancel arch during 19th-century restoration, depict the Crucifixion, St Peter with his key and book, and Christ enthroned. Circular medieval dovecote in the village still with its potence or revolving ladder, used to reach the 550 nesting places. Fragments of Roman slabs showing hooded Celtic deities have been found in Well Field.

**Daylesford** (F6) Daylesford House (1787) was designed by S.P. Cockerell, architect of Sezincote (but not in the same Indian idiom, apart from the top of the dome) for Warren Hastings – Cockerell was architect to the East India Company. Small estate village by the drive. Church (1860) by J.L. Pearson, architect of Truro Cathedral. Hastings' tomb in the graveyard, E of the church, records only his name and the year of his death.

**Didmarton** (B2) The medieval church of St Lawrence, abandoned for a new church in 1872, survives in its 18th century state, now sensitively restored by the Redundant Churches Fund. Towering three-decker pulpit. Box pews and panelling painted the 18th century's favourite pale green. Decalogue over altar brought from a farm where it had been abandoned. Norman font with hand-

*▼ Eastleach Martin: the church stands beside the River Leach in sight of Eastleach Turville church on the opposite bank. In the foreground are the flat paving slabs of Keble Bridge. The church was founded by Richard Fitzpons, one of William the Conqueror's knights. To the left of the tower is the 14th-century north transept: its windows are in the Decorated style, rare in the Cotswolds. The churchyard is full of snowdrops in spring*

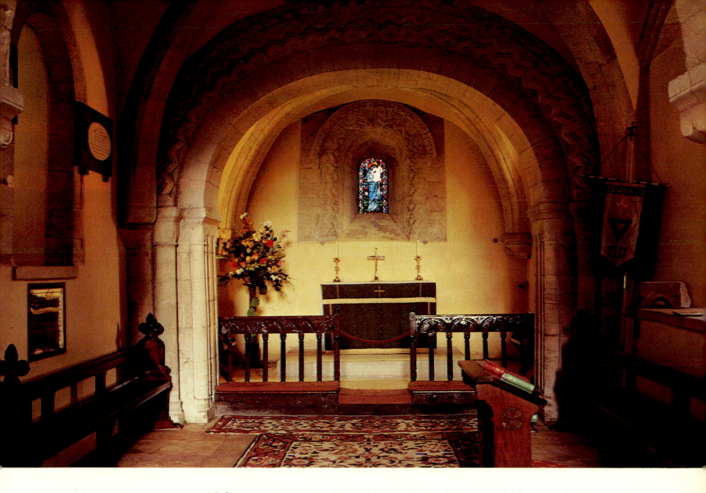

some 18th-century cover. Attractive village with several 18th- and 19th-century stone houses. Nan Tow's Tump, a round barrow, lies 1 mile NE.

**Dodington** (A1)  Dodington Park (open to the public) was begun in 1795 by James Wyatt, a rude and unreliable man but a wildly fashionable architect (he designed Beckford's Fonthill), for Christopher Codrington, who made his fortune in the West Indies. Solemn exterior dominated by the vast colonnade of its portico. Lavishly decorated entrance hall leading to the great staircase. Outbuildings, also by Wyatt, include stables, a dower house and the beautiful domed cruciform Doric church. Capability Brown designed the grounds and the gothick cascade buildings (1764), a castellated tower and waterfall between two lakes.

**Donnington** (E6)  The R. Dikler disappears at Hinchwick and emerges into an artificial lake created for Donnington Mill and now a reservoir for Moreton-in-Marsh and home of ducks and black swans. The 14th-century corn (and later cloth) mill was bought (1827) by Thomas Arkell, who ran three mills, a bakehouse and a malthouse here. Arkell's Donnington Ales (established 1865) is now the Cotswolds' only brewery. The village, 2 miles E, has pretty 17th- and 18th-century cottages.

**Dover's Hill** see **Saintbury**

**Dowdeswell** (C5)  Mainly 14th-century church, set on a hillside and flanked by trees and farm buildings. Evidence of Norman foundation in the tympanum showing the Tree of Life, now on the 19th-century s organ chamber gable. Attractive 16th-century spire with dovecotes let into it. Two galleries approached by private outside doors, on the w for the manor and in the N transept for the rectory. Very fine brass of a priest (c1520) in the chancel.

**Down Ampney** (D3)  The 13th-century church and Down Ampney House (15th century with alterations by Soane, 1799) stand somewhat aloofly at the s end of the straggling village. Church interior darkened by heavy Victorian woodwork. Beautiful nave arcade with lovely leaf carving on the capitals and 13th-century painting of red flowers under the arches. Two excellent monuments: recumbent Sir Nicholas de Valers, wearing the pilgrim's cockleshell, with his wife (early 14th century), in the s transept; and Sir John Hungerford and his son Sir Anthony, both with fine profiles, kneeling opposite each other (1637), in the N transept. Ralph Vaughan Williams was born in the Old Vicarage in 1872; his father was vicar.

**Duntisbourne Abbots** (C4)  One of four Duntisbournes in the tiny valley of the Dun above Daglingworth. A long ford edged with monkey flower fills the road to Duntisbourne Leer. Solemn little church, the tower with a 15th-century saddle-backed roof. In 1875 villagers reinterred Neolithic skeletons from a long barrow, disturbed by ploughing, in the graveyard, adding a cross carved from a slab from nearby Jack Barrow, also destroyed.

**Duntisbourne Leer** (C4)  Named after the Abbey of Lire in Normandy, which owned the manor until 1416. From Roman Ermine Street (A417) the road descends the valley to a ford, surrounded by pretty Cotswold farms with pigeon-holes in their gables, and filled with ducks, wagtails, and the pigeons themselves.

**Duntisbourne Rouse** (C4)  Named after the Rous family, former lords of the manor. The church, on a steep slope rising out of lush pasture, has an Anglo-Saxon nave with attractive 18th-century box pews and panelling, a Jacobean pulpit, 13th-century chancel wall-painting of flowers and trellis-work, and 16th-century choir stalls with misericords bearing lions' heads and vine leaves. At Middle Duntisbourne (NW) 17th-century cottages edge the ford.

**Dursley** (A3)  Town sheltering below the beechwoods of Stinchcombe Hill on the Cotswold edge, granted a market in the 12th century and later an important clothing town; it now houses some of its light industry in the old cloth mills. The church tower (1707–9), replacing one that collapsed in 1698, is a good example of a gothick survival at a late date. Imposing 18th-century buildings include the Market House (1738), with a hipped tile roof, rough-cast whitewashed stone columns, and a statue of Queen Anne in a niche facing the market square. Local legend tells of a supernatural inn providing refuge in stormy weather: travellers awake in the morning to find it vanished.

**Dyrham** (A1)  William Blathwayt, secretary of state to William of Orange, married Mary Wynter, heiress of Dyrham, an Elizabethan manor house in a wooded hollow below the Cotswold edge N of Bath. In 1692 he began to rebuild it and added a new range overlooking a formal Dutch garden (now replaced with lawns). The E range, designed (1698) by William Talman, an assistant of Wren and architect of Chatsworth's E front, faces visitors as they descend the slope through the deer park. This golden baroque exterior contrasts with the interiors, which reflect Blathwayt's love of all things Dutch and, in the blue and white Delftware and leather-hung walls, the taste of the previous generation. Dyrham Park is now a National Trust property. The mid-13th-century church, down a narrow lane behind the mansion, has 15th-century stained glass (E window), a superb memorial brass (1416) to Sir Maurice Russell and his wife and a striking Wynter family monument (1581) with crude lettering.

► *Fairford church: the 15th-century west window, the climax of a superb series of stained glass windows unrivalled in any English parish church, shows the Last Judgement. At the top is Christ in glory, his feet resting on the earth, which glows red in the fires of the end of the world. On either side of his head are scrolls bearing the words 'Justice' and 'Mercy'. Left is the Virgin and right St John the Baptist; angels and saints circle about them. In the lower half St Michael stands directly below Christ, holding the scales of judgement and a processional cross, in the midst of a fight between angels and devils for the judged souls. Left of St Michael the blessed ascend to heaven; at the bottom right luridly coloured demons drag the damned down to the flames of hell*

**Eastleach Martin** and **Eastleach Turville** (E4) Villages either side of the R. Leach, each with its own church, connected by Keble's Bridge, a bridge of flat paving stones named after the family who once held Eastleach Turville manor. From the river, bordered with daffodils in spring and meadowsweet and codlins-and-cream in summer, a path leads to Eastleach Martin church, set in front of a wooded slope – perhaps the most memorably picturesque scene in the entire Cotswolds. Eastleach Turville church has a 14th-century saddle-backed tower, a s doorway of *c*1130 with a carved tympanum of Christ in majesty in a mandorla supported by angels, and a very fine 13th-century chancel with triple lancets in its E wall.

**Ebrington** (E8), locally sometimes called Yabberton, has a reputation for particularly slow-witted inhabitants: many stories are told, e.g. of their attempt to make their church tower grow by manuring its base. The church, dedicated to King Alfred's granddaughter St Eadburga, has a Norman s doorway with a diapered tympanum. The painted effigy of Sir John Fortescue, Lord Chief Justice under Henry VI, on his tomb on the chancel's N side, shows him in his legal robes. Several thatched cottages in the village.

**Elkstone** (C5) Famous for its glorious Norman church, begun *c*1160. In the 13th century a central tower collapsed or was taken down, the chancel roof was raised to the height of the nave and the extra space was made into a dovecote, reached by a staircase near the pulpit. The present tall and stately tower, *c*1370, has buttresses adorned with gargoyles and grotesque figures playing musical instruments. On the nave exterior is a series of corbels of animals, birds and signs of the zodiac. The s doorway tympanum shows Christ in majesty, with witty beakhead ornament on the surrounding arch. Inside, two arches show the

*▲ Fairford church: the 15th-century tower, showing details of the lavish carvings with which the wool merchants ornamented their great church. On its west side is a late-15th-century sculpture of Christ, carved in a deliberately archaic style. The figure clutching a sword is one of four that guard each angle of the tower; above him is a padlock*

position of the original tower; the space between was vaulted in the 14th century. The sanctuary has a Norman vault whose ribs meet in the centre at four grotesque heads buckled together. The graveyard, thickly edged with trees, contains fine 17th-century table tombs carved with cherubs and skulls and crossbones. 18th-century rectory, at the end of a drive beside the church.

**Fairford** (E4) Handsome market town with a magnificent church renowned for its stained glass. 6th-century Saxons in the Thames valley began their penetration of the Cotswolds by establishing a cemetery here. The medieval cloth trade brought prosperity; the chief citizens in the 15th century, the Tame family, undertook the rebuilding of the entire church from 1480 (tomb of John Tame and his wife between the chancel and Lady Chapel). Grotesque figures from the old church were placed on the new central tower. Spacious interior, well lit by its large windows and clerestory. Roof supported by 69 angel corbels. The chancel has much woodwork, rare in the Cotswolds: finely carved screens and choir stalls. The late medieval stained glass is excelled in England only by that of a royal foundation – King's College, Cambridge (slightly later), where some of the same Flemish and English artists worked. The single scheme begins on the N side outside the Lady Chapel screen and shows (reading clockwise) Old Testament prefigurations of Christ, the life of the Virgin, the events of Christ's life and his Resurrection. In the nave the 12 apostles (s) face the prophets (all carrying corresponding texts from the Old and New Testaments), evangelists and doctors of the Church. In the N clerestory, very glum persecutors and traitors of the Church with ghoulish demons in the tracery lights above them; opposite, saints and martyrs with angels. The w window (blown in by a gale in 1703 and carefully replaced) is an intensely dramatic depiction of the Last Judgement. Several good 17th-century table tombs in the churchyard include, near the s porch, that of Valentine Strong, master mason of Taynton,

*▼ Fairford church is unusual among Cotswold churches in retaining a considerable quantity of good early woodwork. The choir stalls, dating from the reign of Henry VII, have 14 carved misericords; this one shows a fox stealing geese*

founder of the family who worked for Wren on St Paul's – a typical 'bale' tomb, i.e. having a semicylindrical top carved with grooves, popularly supposed to represent bales of cloth, but more likely intended as a hearse. High Street leads from the church to the market place. Dignified grey stone houses and inns (17th and 18th century). The Coln water meadows, popular with fishermen and cows and skimmed by swallows and martins, give rural tranquillity to the s of the town. Concorde sweeps past from its nearby base.

**Gatcombe Park** see **Avening**

**Great Badminton** see **Badminton**

**Great Barrington** (E5) Barrington quarries supplied stone for many Cotswold churches and houses, and for the rebuilding of churches in the City of London after the Great Fire. The village stands outside the beautiful wrought-iron gates of Palladian Barrington Park (1736–8) and overlooks its landscaped park, through which the Windrush flows. Imposing Norman church, tamed by the Victorians. Richly carved 12th-century chancel arch. Monuments to Mary, Countess Talbot, by Nollekens (1787), to the Bray children (1720: 'She died at her Aunt Catchmay's . . . He dyed at the Royal Academy of Angiers') and of Captain Edmund Bray in armour (1620), with his sword on his right side, because Queen Elizabeth pardoned him for a murder and he vowed in gratitude never again to use his offending right hand (or so the story goes; he may of course simply have been left-handed).

**Great Rissington** (E5) The visitor travelling from Bourton-on-the-Water sees the village attractively spread out on the hillside opposite. Much altered 12th-century cruciform church. Tower with 15th-century upper stages. The porch contains a reset 15th-century carved stone panel showing the Crucifixion. 17th-century manor house and 18th-century rectory.

▼ *Hailes: a detail of the wall-painting (c1300) in the chancel of the 12th-century church, above a 14th-century window. A basilisk (right), whose look kills, faces a griffon, which has the head and wings of an eagle and the body of a lion. The grids flanking the window contain the heraldic devices of Richard, Earl of Cornwall (founder of Hailes Abbey), and his family; the lion is the device of his third wife, Beatrice von Falkenstein*

**Guiting Power** (D6) Spacious village, its cottages scattered round a large green. Church with Norman N and S doorways and 13th-century nave roof.

**Hailes** (D6) Extremely interesting church, built *c*1139–51 and later acquired by the neighbouring, and now ruined, Cistercian abbey. 13th-century tiles and 15th-century stained glass, taken from the abbey ruins. Fittings mainly intact. 15th-century rood screen. Pre-Reformation pews. In the 17th century the altar was moved away from the E wall in conformity with Puritan practice. 17th-century sanctuary panelling. Delightful wall-paintings (*c*1300), financed by the abbey's patrons. Censing angels amid roses either side of the E window probably formed part of a total design with the stained glass, which may have depicted the Virgin. On the splays of half-blocked Norman windows (chancel N wall) are astonishingly well-preserved paintings of St Catherine and St Margaret, with monks kneeling beside them. Nave paintings, uncovered in 1970, show (N wall) St Christopher and (S wall) a hunting scene, a subject often illustrated in medieval manuscripts and here perhaps portraying Sampson the Venour, Edward I's huntsman and a pensioner of the abbey. Three lean and muscular hounds leap towards a terrified hare crouching under a bare and thorny bush; behind them the huntsman blows his horn.

Richard, Earl of Cornwall and later King of the Romans, founded the Cistercian Abbey of Hailes in 1251 (in fulfilment of a vow made during a storm off the Scilly Isles) on land given him by his brother, Henry III. In 1270 his son Edmund gave the abbey a phial of Christ's blood, which was splendidly enshrined and made Hailes a major centre of pilgrimage (mentioned by

Chaucer in *The Canterbury Tales*). In 1538, when all English shrines were suppressed, the Bishop of Rochester publicly displayed the relic in London and said it was merely saffron-coloured honey. The Crown sold the abbey (1542) and it was demolished. The ruins – the cloister is the only substantial part left above ground – have an attractive rural setting, surrounded by trees against the backdrop of Salter's Hill. A museum on the site contains fragments of tiles, glass and masonry found during excavation. Cistercians had to live apart from all human habitation, so the village of Hailes was moved when the abbey was built, probably to Didbrook, 1 mile N.

**Hampnett** (D5) Secluded gated village of scattered cottages and large barns dotted on unfenced grazing land. Good views of Northleach church tower from the graveyard entrance. Norman church in three sections, as at Elkstone: nave, chancel which once carried a tower, and sanctuary, vaulted like Elkstone's and an equally fine example of late Norman architecture, with excellent carving of doves on the capitals. *c*1871 the chancel and sanctuary were painted by the vicar, the Rev. Wiggin, aided by Clayton & Bell, the firm that produced the best pre-Morris Victorian stained glass, including the E window here. Later Hampnett invited visitors to subscribe to a fund for the removal of its paintings which fortunately never raised enough money, and now this attempt to imitate the decoration that existed in all medieval churches is once more appreciated, thanks to the revived interest in the ecclesiastical art of Morris and his circle. The colours are mostly subdued russets and blues and create an impression of richness which is not overpowering. Hangman's Stone, a Bronze Age monolith, stands at the meeting-point of the parishes of Yanworth, Stowell and Hampnett (junction of A40 and the Stowell road).

*Two outstanding Cotswold gardens: below, Hidcote Manor garden (designed by Major Johnston, who acquired the manor in 1905), notable for its use of hedges to divide a large area into small intimate spaces, creating a succession of 'cottage' gardens; and (right) the Georgian façade of Kiftsgate Court, whose gardens, laid out in the 1920s, are famous for* Rosafilipes-Kiftsgate, *a rambler rose which grows up to 18 m high*

**Harnhill** (D4)  Norman church of St Michael, with s doorway tympanum of St Michael fighting the dragon. 17th-century rectory gothickised 1810. Tudor manor house with 18th-century façade and a summerhouse that was formerly a dovecote.

**Hatherop** (E4), like Coln St Aldwyns and Quenington, lies on the edge of the lovely parkland of Williamstrip, a late-17th-century mansion perhaps built for Henry Powle, speaker of the House of Commons. Largely 19th-century estate village. Church (1854–5) and castle (1850–6) rebuilt for Lord de Mauley by Henry Clutton, whose assistant, William Burges, the most opulently decorative Victorian architect-artist (see Cardiff Castle), was responsible for the vigorous carving on the church. Monument to Barbara, Lady de Mauley, by Raffaele Monti (1848): she lies in death upon the tomb with angels at her head and feet; very lush.

**Hidcote** (E8)  Two hamlets, Hidcote Boyce and Hidcote Bartrim, within the parish of Ebrington. Between them is beautiful Hidcote House (1663), of golden ashlar, with stepped ogee gables. Hidcote Bartrim's late-17th-century manor has famous gardens, now owned by the National Trust.

**Highgrove** see **Tetbury**

**Hinchwick** see **Condicote**

**Kelmscott** (F4)  Remote rural, almost primitive, village nearly in the Thames valley but included here for its associations with William Morris, who pioneered appreciation of the Cotswolds. Kelmscott Manor, his country home 1871–96, was restored in 1968 (open to the public for a few days each year), its rooms decorated according to his tastes, with white-painted woodwork and his

wallpapers, fabrics, carpets and tapestries (some woven here). William de Morgan tiles. Pictures by Burne-Jones and Rossetti, many of Morris' wife Janey. Books from the Kelmscott Press, and furniture designed by Ford Madox Brown, in the attics. Morris is buried in the SE corner of the churchyard, under a tomb with beautiful but badly weathered lettering. The church, mostly 12th and 13th century, has 14th-century wall-paintings of figures under trefoiled arches. Village Hall (1928–34) designed by Ernest Gimson. Morris Cottages (1902), built at the expense of Morris' widow, have a relief of Morris sitting under a tree in the home mead behind the manor.

**Kiftsgate** (E8) Kiftsgate Court's famous gardens (open to the public) were begun in the 18th century when Walwyn Graves modernised Mickleton House, his small Elizabethan manor, with a Georgian façade and an elm avenue leading uphill to where Kiftsgate now stands. In 1887 his descendant decided that the view from the top was so good that the house should really be there, so he had a railway constructed to move the Georgian façade up the escarpment and added it to his big new house, Kiftsgate Court. The denuded manor house is now a school.

**Kineton** see **Temple Guiting**

**Lechlade** (E4) Highest navigable point of the Thames, junction of the Coln and Leach on the southern border of the Cotswolds near the end of the Thames and Severn Canal. Much week-end pleasure boating (a marina occupies old wharves near Halfpenny Bridge). 18th- and early-19th-century houses surround the market place. 15th–16th-century church, one of the Cotswolds' best wool churches. Airy and well-lit interior. Superb chancel roof decorated with carved bosses, of angels bearing the instruments of the Passion and (rather incongruously) of men wrestling. In 1815 Shelley, on a rowing trip with Mary Godwin, Peacock and Charles Clairmont from Windsor to the source of the Thames, spent the night at Lechlade and wrote 'Stanzas in a Summer Evening Churchyard'; lines from the poem have been inscribed in a stone at the beginning of 'Shelley's Walk' from the church to the river.

**Little Badminton** see **Badminton**

**Little Barrington** (E5) Cottages spread around a rather wild grassy hollow (a former quarry) in the slope down to the R. Windrush. The church has a superbly preserved 12th-century s doorway with deeply cut ornament on the piers, crisply carved foliage in the capitals and a hideous head at the top. A beautiful Norman tympanum, once over a N doorway and now set into the N outer wall of the aisle, shows Christ in majesty supported by two angels, each with a wing poised delicately behind Christ's haloed head to make a canopy. Especially fine carving of the drapery, particularly below Christ's knees.

**Little Rissington** (E6) Village by a little brook running down to the Windrush. Views across the valley to the flooded gravel pits E of Bourton-on-the-Water. The church, in fields to the N, considerably rebuilt by the Victorians, retains its 12th-century nave arcade and 13th-century chancel. Many substantial farm buildings in the centre of the village and, despite the nearby RAF station, an undisturbed rural atmosphere.

**Lodge Park** see **Sherborne**

**Lower Slaughter** (E6), one of the most famously picturesque villages in England, never the scene of a massacre, probably derives its name from Anglo-Saxon *sloh*, 'mire', or possibly *slah treow*, 'sloe tree'. Pretty cottages with luxuriant gardens grouped around a green on the N side of a brook spanned by

▼ *Minchinhampton, in the less-frequented south-western Cotswolds: the Market House (1698), built on stone columns with a row of wooden pillars in the middle*

clapper bridges. Massive gate-piers lead to the 17th-century manor house with a 16th-century dovecote that looks like a giant Tudor doll's-house.

**Lower Swell** (E6; also called Nether Swell) Attractive village on a busy road (A436), edged on the E by the R. Dikler, which also runs past Abbotswood, a large country house (1902) by Lutyens NE of the village, with famous water and flower gardens occasionally open to the public. NW of the village (on private land) is the greatest concentration of long barrows in the Cotswolds and several Bronze Age round barrows. Norman church: 12th-century nave, now the s aisle of a Victorian nave. Chancel (1870) with attractive wall-paintings by Clayton & Bell (who also did all the stained glass) illustrating the story of the Passion in subdued warm tones, predominantly ochre and terracotta. The Norman tympanum over the s door has an apparently unfinished carving of a dove pecking at fruit on the Tree of Life. Even more pagan in feeling are the 18 carvings round the old chancel arch: a continuous band divided into boxes crudely carved with mannikins (hacked by disapproving later centuries?), apples(?), interlinked rings, three fish, a hare, a salamander and other devices. Carvings on the capitals show people and serpents. The symbolism, if any, has never been satisfactorily explained; the uneasy Christian interpretation offered by the church in its leaflet does not convince.

**Lypiatt** see **Bisley**

**Marshfield** (A1), a large village on light soil on top of a hill, probably derives its name from 'maeres field', a tract of open border land. The long High Street with several 18th-century houses and inns gives a small-town feel. The cloth trade caused rapid growth in the 15th century, when the small Norman church was almost entirely replaced (1470); the present impressive building contains

*▼ North Cerney, a delightful and beautifully cared-for village in the Churn valley. The lower stages of the church tower are Norman; its upper storey was added c1200. The saddle-backed roof was erected after a fire gutted the church in the 15th century. Also visible is the north transept of 1490*

monuments to the Webbs, Marshfield's leading clothier family. The 17th-century manor house N of the church has fine outbuildings, notably a circular dovecote and massive barn.

**Meysey Hampton** (E4) Neat village with a Georgian manor house overlooking the green. The church (consecrated 1269), probably financed by the Knights Templar, has a very fine chancel, enlarged and enriched in the 14th century. Beautiful E window with ball-flower ornament in its external mouldings. s are four crocketed canopies above the sedilia (priests' seats) and piscina (basin for washing communion vessels) next to a tomb recess, all excellently carved. Large monument (1626) in the s transept to James Vaulx and his two wives, who are strikingly differently portrayed – the deceased idealised, the living unflatteringly shown to have a double chin, fat face and lank hair.

**Middle Duntisbourne** see **Duntisbourne Rouse**

**Minchinhampton** (B4) Beautiful small market town made prosperous by the cloth trade; built entirely of local grey limestone. Market House of 1698. Queen Anne Post Office. Numerous good 17th- and 18th-century houses in the High Street and the little side streets that run downhill straight into countryside. Church rebuilt 12th and (except its transepts) 19th centuries. Curious spire, truncated in 1563. The s transept is the Cotswolds' best example of the Decorated style, with the upper part of the s window in the form of a rose and an exquisite arched roof, almost like a design for timber executed in stone. John of Ansley and his wife Lucy, the donors, are lavishly entombed here. William Halliday's memorial, one of several fine brasses, includes his wool merchant's mark. Minchinhampton Common, N of the town, 580 acres of exposed downland grazed by horses, cattle, and sheep, is National Trust property. 1 mile w of

the church are The Bulwarks, a rampart and ditch nearly 1 mile long – remains of an Iron Age fortress from the Roman invasion (*c*AD 43). The longstone on the common, part of a vanished long barrow, has a hole in it, traditionally with curative powers. Tom Long's Signpost at the meeting-point of six roads across the common is named after a highwayman who was gibbetted there.

**Miserden** (C4)  Estate cottages on the edge of Misarden Park, a 17th-century mansion extended in the 19th century by Waterhouse and in the 20th by Lutyens. The park's private woodland contains the motte and bailey of a castle built by the Musard family (who gave their name to the village) soon after 1066 and abandoned in the 13th century. Church basically Saxon but heavily restored. On William Kingston's monument (1614) a goat eats a cabbage at his feet. The war memorial in the beech- and yew-filled churchyard is by Lutyens.

**Moreton-in-Marsh** (E7), originally called Morton Henmarsh, in a water-logged plain, was founded in the 13th century by the Abbot of Westminster to exploit the junction of the Fosse Way and the Worcester Road (A44); numerous hotels, inns and restaurants along the wide and always busy main street emphasise that the town was created to cater for travellers, and still does. The oldest building, the 16th-century tower at the corner of Oxford Street, has a clock dated 1648 and a bell used for the curfew until 1860. Market Hall (1887) given by Lord Redesdale. Church rebuilt 1858. Fine 18th-century façades, notably St David's House, E of the church.

**Nailsworth** (B3)  Industrial town in a dramatic valley s of Stroud (in places the hill rising out of the town, the Nailsworth Ladder, has a gradient of almost 1 in 2). A rather bitty centre, with some attractive houses tucked away in side streets. The early and beautiful Quaker Meeting House (1689) retains its original panelling and seating. Mills on the road to Stroud provide the chief architectural interest: Dunkirk Mills, the largest in the area (18th century, repeatedly enlarged in the cloth boom 1800–20); Egypt Mills, with a fine 18th-century mill house; Inchbrook Mill, now a private home; and Dunkirk Mill, now occupied by five separate firms. 18th- and 19th-century clothiers' houses on the hillsides.

**Naunton** (D6) follows the Windrush valley for a mile. Its famous dovecote (*c*1600), badly decayed, has four gables, making it look like a small cottage. The church, at the w end of the village, is of beautiful golden limestone, as are many of the cottages, and is given a very rural feel by the rough pasture rising straight up behind. Largely rebuilt in the 16th century, it has a 17th-century tower with gargoyles and grotesques. Its greatest treasure is the richly carved pulpit (*c*1400). Old Rectory (1694) SE of the church.

**North Cerney** (D4) Village in the Churn valley. The beauty of the church, originally 12th century, is largely due to 20th-century restoration and refurnishing. Much rebuilding 1465–70, after a fire which gutted the nave and tower. Transepts added 1483 (s, a Lady Chapel) and 1490 (N, chapel of St Catherine). s doorway with diapered tympanum and four weird little heads butting into the design. 15th-century nave roof, carried on the N wall by three large bold corbel heads representing (probably) the rector at the time of rebuilding, Henry VI, and the Duke of Buckingham (it is appropriate that only his head is shown – it was cut off by Richard III). 18th-century gallery, reached by an external staircase. Magnificent pulpit (*c*1480) of wine-glass form, a slim shaft spreading to form a base for the richly decorated bowl, carved from a single block of stone.

▼ *A corner of Painswick's famous churchyard, with some of the 99 yews and a selection of the elaborate tombs, mostly 17th and 18th century: the cylindrical variety is known locally as 'tea caddy'. In the background (left) is The Beacon, one of the finest of the many excellent 18th-century houses in the town*

15th-century stained glass in the Lady Chapel's E window. 15th-century continental statues of the Virgin and two bishops and, on the modern rood loft, an Italian crucifix (c1600), all placed here during 20th-century renovation. Opposite the church is the Old Rectory (1694), a handsome building with a hipped roof.

**Northleach** (D5) Important Cotswold market town on the busy A40, made wealthy by the cloth trade. Local clothiers financed its imposing church (15th century), whose lofty tower is visible for miles around. The very beautiful S porch, unusually retaining its medieval images – the Virgin, the Trinity, John the Baptist and Thomas à Becket – is elegantly vaulted and has carved image brackets, one a cat fiddling to three rats. Nave with octagonal concave piers and capitals, as at Chipping Campden and presumably by the same mason. The timber roofs are the original ones. Late-14th-century font, carved with demons defeated by baptism and angels playing musical instruments. Modern seating designed by Sir Basil Spence, architect of Coventry Cathedral. Outstanding collection of memorial brasses of merchant benefactors, e.g. the Bicknells, who gave the Lady Chapel. The prison (on the A40/Fosse Way crossroads), built 1789–91 by Sir Onesiphorous Paul, a pioneer of prison reform, is now a museum of Cotswold agricultural life.

**Notgrove** (D6) Upland village, its cottages spread around a shaggy green. Church of Norman origin, supposedly on the site of a Saxon cemetery. Disturbingly primitive Saxon carving of the Crucifixion in an exterior niche on the E wall. 14th-century N transept, the window with ball-flower ornament. Pretty octagonal tower, probably also 14th century. Narrow nave with impressive Norman arcade. Norman font with cable-moulding below its brim. Three 16th- and 17th-century effigies in the chancel of the Whittington family, descendants of the great wool merchant Dick Whittington.

**Oddington** (F6) Site of a Civil War battle (1643) in which Prince Rupert was defeated. The old church (abandoned 1852), in an isolated and idyllic situation amongst trees and surrounded by fields at the end of a long lane running SE towards Bledington, remains rustic and unspoilt. 13th-century nave, chancel and tower. The S aisle (12th century) was originally the nave. Stone seats in the 14th-century porch have grooves (caused by local men sharpening their arrows) beside the puzzling outlines of two feet. A magnificent 14th-century Doom painting fills the nave N wall. Christ sits in judgement at the top; angels blow trumpets to summon the dead; the good are handed up into paradise (castellated towers) while devils (one with smart stripes) drag the damned into hell – one fans the flames with bellows. Richly carved Jacobean pulpit, still with its sounding board: local tradition says that a vixen once raised her cubs in it.

**Owlpen** (A3) A secret and romantic place on a steep, thickly wooded slope. The gabled 15th-century manor house (extended 16th–18th centuries) has terraced gardens, neatly clipped yews and a gazebo, and forms a perfect picturesque Cotswold group with the little Victorian church perched above, the 18th-century mill, and the medieval barn.

**Ozleworth** (A3) At the top of a deep secluded valley stands Ozleworth Park, a dignified 18th-century house with Regency additions. The very fine Norman church behind it is in the middle of a circular plot, perhaps a Bronze Age henge monument and a site of ancient sanctity. Its oldest part is a central hexagonal tower, extremely rare. Nave added and font installed early 13th century; chancel extended 14th century.

**Painswick** (B4) Attractive small town built almost entirely of silvery-grey stone and beautifully set between two steep valleys. The narrow streets are a pleasure to explore (though usually choked with traffic), having a wealth of good domestic architecture, mostly 17th and 18th century, e.g. Court House (c1604), s of the church, built for the clothier Thomas Gardner; The Beacon, the best 18th-century house, N of the churchyard; Loveday's House (18th century) in St Mary's Street; and Yew Tree House (c1668) in Vicarage Lane. Older buildings include New Hall, a 15th-century cloth hall on the corner of New Street. Many of the stone façades conceal earlier timber frames – in the case of the Post Office, strikingly revealed.

Painswick church has a glorious 17th-century spire, late-14th-century doorway and 15th-century tower and nave. St Peter's Chapel (c1378, the earliest part of the church) contains the tomb of Anne Boleyn's gaoler, Sir William Kingston, on a 15th-century tomb-chest. During the Civil War Parliamentarian troops were discovered hiding in the church from Charles I's army (in retreat after failing to capture Gloucester), and the Royalist general Sir William Vavasour broke in 'firing the doors and casting in hand grenades' (which is probably when Sir William Kingston's tomb-chest was burnt). The graveyard is famous for its 18th-century clipped yews. There are supposed to be 99; according to tradition, if more are planted they will wither (some have suffered badly in recent snows). They form an effective foil to the Cotswolds' finest assemblage of tombs. John Bryan designed many of them, and also the NE gateway; his own remarkable tomb (1787) is a pyramid, a miniature version of the tomb of Caius Cestius in Rome. The yews are clipped every 19 September and on the following Sunday there is a church-clipping ceremony, with a service and special hymn, after which children encircle the church and dance – an ancient custom formerly practised at many churches in England and abroad. 'Puppy-dog pie', a plum pie containing a small china dog, is traditionally made for the day, supposedly in memory of pies made with real dogs for the crowds at the church-clipping, but perhaps dimly recalling sacrifices made when the clipping was a pagan dance round an outdoor altar.

Painswick House (½ mile N, open to the public), a distinguished 18th-century mansion with wings by George Basevi (1830), was called Buenos Ayres by its first owner, Charles Hyett, who chose the site because of its healthy air and had the ground-floor reception rooms built with specially high ceilings to help his asthmatic breathing. Hyetts still own the house but its interior decoration is largely by the lessee, the Baroncino de Piro. Numerous outbuildings include a lovely octagonal dovecote. Many of the substantial 17th- and 18th-century houses on the outskirts of Painswick were built for clothiers, next to their mills. Brook House Mills, mostly 18th and 19th century, s of the town on the Painswick stream, had the last working water wheel of any Cotswold cloth mill, stopped in 1962; the machinery it powered was then making hairpins.

**Postlip** (C6) sw of Winchcombe, at the foot of the slope leading down from Cleeve Common. Postlip Hall, a beautiful Tudor manor house, has a 15th-century tithe barn and, on its lawns, St James' Chapel, a small Norman church (now Roman Catholic) reputedly built by the lord of the manor because the Barons' War had left the countryside so lawless that his servants dared not venture out to the parish church. At one time used as a barn, it has a decorated s doorway and chancel arch and 16th-century nave roof.

**Prinknash** (B5, pronounced 'Prinnidge') Prinknash Abbey clings to the

▶*Rendcomb: the superb Norman font shows the 11 loyal apostles standing below a Romanesque arcade between bands of unusual key ornament at the top and stylised honeysuckle decoration beneath. The twelfth space, nearest the pillar, has an uncarved surface in place of Judas. The background gives a glimpse of the church's fine wooden screens, rare in the Cotswolds; they were donated by Sir Edmund Tame of Fairford, who financed the rebuilding of this church*

beech-clad Cotswold edge, with superb views over the Severn plain. The oldest part (14th century), originally a grange and hunting lodge for the Abbot of Gloucester, was largely rebuilt by the last abbot c1514. After the Dissolution it was owned by Lord Chandos of Sudeley and in 1643 was occupied by Prince Rupert. The Benedictines acquired it in 1928; their new building, delayed by the war, was finally opened in 1972. Many of the fittings, including the chapel's fine stained glass, were made by the monks, who run a well-known pottery here.

**Quenington** (E4) Delightful village in the Coln valley. The 14th-century gatehouse and dovecote of the Knights Hospitaller's community (founded 12th century) survive in the grounds of 19th-century Quenington Court. The church, near the river beside a mill, is famous for its two magnificent doorways (12th century). Each has a carved tympanum, showing (N) the harrowing of hell and (S) the coronation of the Virgin – the earliest known representation, with the possible exception of a capital from Reading Abbey, of this subject in Western European art. Next to the Virgin are seraphim and the symbols of St John and St Luke; next to Christ, the symbols of St Matthew and St Mark and a little temple, probably the celestial Jerusalem.

**Rendcomb** (D4) Superbly situated in woodland in the steep Churn valley. The village is dominated by Rendcomb College (once a country house, now a boys' school), designed by Philip Hardwick – a vast and opulently Italianate mansion and no less impressive stables, with a French-looking tall central tower. Fine early-16th-century church (also the school chapel), financed by Sir Edmund Tame, whose father donated the somewhat similar Fairford church, and like Fairford retaining most of its wooden screens, rare in the Cotswolds.

▼ *The Rollright Stones, a Bronze Age standing circle. Of the original 11 stones several have been broken up, their fragments erected on the perimeter. According to tradition they are impossible to count: a baker is said to have attempted the task by putting a loaf of bread on each stone, but as he rounded the circle he found that the first loaves had disappeared – a story which perhaps incorporates the memory of a time when offerings were made at the stones.*

▲ *The road to Salperton.*
*Two 18th-century changes*
*in the Cotswold landscape*
*can be seen here, both the*
*result of a shift from sheep*
*rearing to arable*
*farming: a row of*
*beeches, planted as a*
*windbreak to prevent*
*erosion of the thin light*
*soil, and one of the dry*
*stone walls erected to*
*break up the great sheep-*
*runs into fields*

Surviving fragments suggest the original beauty of the stained glass. Outstandingly fine Norman font, probably brought from Elmore, Gloucestershire, by the Guise family, formerly lords of the manor. Some of them are entombed in the s chapel, which has a pretty 18th-century wrought-iron screen round it incorporating their crest, a swan.

**Rollright Stones** (F7) w of the A34 between Great and Little Rollright, in three separate groups: a stone circle 30 m across, almost certainly a temple; an outlying stone to the N, 2½ m high, the King Stone, probably directional, leading to the circle; and (¼ mile w) the Whispering Knights, four uprights with a capstone now resting partly on the ground – part of a former long barrow which has lost its covering cairn. The knights are Neolithic, the others Bronze Age, i.e. a thousand years later, and many legends are associated with them. A king was said to have approached the site as he set out with his army to conquer England, whereupon the witch who owned it appeared and said, 'Seven long strides shalt thou take;/If Long Compton thou canst see,/King of England shalt thou be.' The king, being only a few paces from the crest of the hill overlooking the village, confidently replied, 'Stick, stock, stone,/As King of England I shall be known'; but he found his view of Long Compton blocked by the mound of earth which still stands in front of the King Stone. The witch declared, 'As Long Compton thou canst not see,/King of England thou shalt not be./Rise up, stick, and stand still, stone,/For King of England thou shalt be none;/Thou and thy men hoar stones shall be,/And I myself an eldern tree.' The king and his army turned to stone, as did a group of his knights who had withdrawn to plot treason and who whisper still, foretelling the future. Thick clumps of elder grow near the stones: elder was traditionally supposed to be a witch in disguise because it 'bleeds' when cut, and in former times local people reportedly stood in a circle round the King Stone on midsummer eve to see it nod its head when the elder was cut – a promise of the time when the witch's power would break and the king ride on to conquer England.

**Saintbury** (D7) Village on the scarp edge. Attractive church with Norman nave doorways, 14th-century chancel, 18th-century font cover and box pews, and splendid views from the porch. Dover's Hill, 1 mile w, affording good walks through open fields (National Trust property), is famous for the Cotswold Games, founded in the early 17th century by Robert Dover to maintain traditional Whitsun sports and carnivals in the face of increasing Puritan disapproval, with enthusiastic support from the local gentry – including Endymion Porter of Aston-sub-Edge, who publicised them with a book of celebratory verse contributed to by Drayton, Heywood and Jonson. The main events, held in the hill's natural amphitheatre, were wrestling, dancing, horse racing and (most notoriously) shin-kicking, still practised locally in the 19th century, when training involved toughening the shins by beating them with planks of wood – because the kicking was done with iron-tipped boots. The Games ended in 1851, partly because of enclosures and partly because they had become too rowdy; recently there has been a revival (though shin-kicking still awaits its renaissance).

**Salperton** (D6) A right of way in front of the classical main block of Salperton Park (1817) leads to the church with a Norman nave and chancel (chancel arch *c*1120) and a medieval wall-painting (left of the tower arch, above one of the two

*▼ Sapperton is beautifully situated in steep wooded valleys east of Stroud. The church's central tower and spire and the roofs of the nave and chancel are 14th century; the rest was rebuilt early in the 18th century. The graveyard is filled with lichen-covered tombstones, many containing fossils*

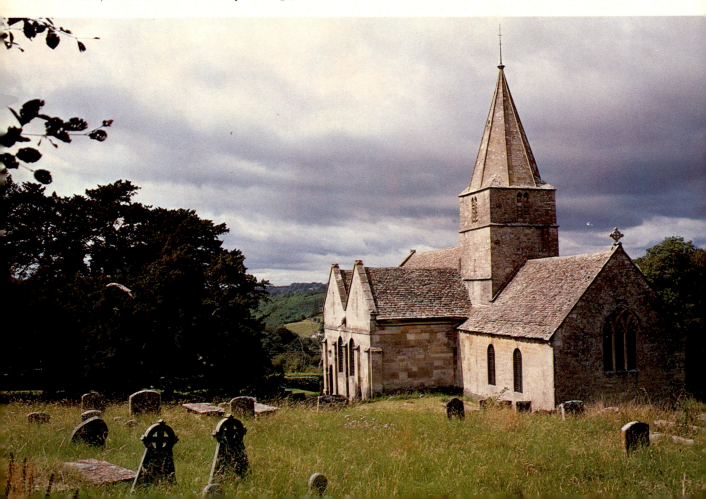

harmoniums) of a skeleton (Death) carrying a scythe, arrow, shroud and shovel. View from the porch of Salperton Park's s wing, the original 17th-century house, five-gabled with a three-gabled extension. The village, ¼ mile N, consists mostly of well-kept 17th- and 18th-century estate cottages.

**Sapperton** (C4), gloriously situated on a ridge above wooded valleys, has an almost alpine feel. Church with classical round-headed nave windows, indicating its extensive 18th-century rebuilding. Jacobean oak cornice in the nave, carved figures on the pew-ends and the flamboyant front of the gallery and s transept panelling – all from Sapperton House, demolished by Lord Bathurst c1730. Two opulent monuments: to Sir Henry Poole, kneeling with his family under a canopy (1616, N transept), and Sir Robert Atkyns, author of a famous history of Gloucestershire, who reclines in a pavilion, book to hand (1711, s transept). Many tombs in the churchyard have brass memorial plates, several 17th century, used because the local stone weathers so severely. Handsome village with cottages by the craftsmen Ernest Gimson and the Barnsley brothers (buried in the churchyard), who used Daneway House, an early medieval manor secluded in woods w of Sapperton, as a workshop, employing the skills of local men for their hand-made furniture.

**Sezincote** (E7) Country house remodelled 1805 in Indian style by Samuel Pepys Cockerell, brother of the owner (Sir Charles Cockerell, who made his fortune in the East India Company), aided by Thomas Daniell, an Indian artist. It influenced the Prince Regent's choice of design for the Brighton Pavilion – he was a visitor here, probably in 1807. The exotic architecture contrasts weirdly with acres of very English parkland. Beautiful gardens surround a stream which curves away from the house downhill to a pool, with

many Indian architectural details, e.g. a 'shrine' at the head of the stream and Brahmin bulls on the Indian bridge. Particularly clever is the choice of familiar English plants arranged to give an oriental appearance, seen to best advantage in subdued light – few gardens can look so attractive in the rain.

**Sheepscombe** (B4) Typical large 18th-century weavers' village. Mills and cottages scattered over a spectacularly steep hillside and surrounded by dense beechwoods. The picturesque green was once the site of gallows erected by Sir Anthony Kingston, Painswick's lord of the manor, a thoroughly nasty royal lackey notorious for his cruelty towards participants in uprisings against Henry VIII and Edward VI protesting against enclosures (he also built Painswick's prison). To make sure that the gallows was not neglected he gave three estates, one to maintain it, one to provide its ladders and one to provide its noose; and he made the tithe-collector the hangman.

**Sherborne** (E5) Sherborne House, a large rather heavy 17th-century building which is now a school, has an uncared-for look. Church (joined by a corridor to the house) rebuilt in the 19th century by Lord Sherborne, except for its tower and spire of *c*1300; it contains several good 18th-century monuments. Attractive row of cottages (one the Post Office) with long front gardens at the E end of the village. The traveller on the obscure road through nondescript country 2 miles SW is surprised by the sophisticated charm of Lodge Park, a 17th-century pavilion of Sherborne House, built for John Dutton as a grandstand for watching deer coursed by dogs in the park.

**Siddington** Village suburb SE of Cirencester (D4). Church of St Peter with a very well preserved Norman S doorway, whose richly carved beakhead sur-

*▲Sezincote: the house (completed 1805) was modelled on Indian mogul designs. Left of the main block is the curved orangery; in front is the Indian garden laid out in 1965 with a canal and Irish yews (a cold-climate substitute for cypresses). 'Sezincote' means 'hillside of oaks', and oaks are still plentiful in the very English surrounding parkland. The village was swept away by enclosures; the church was demolished in 1638*

round resembles Elkstone's s door and is topped by a grotesque head. Tympanum of Christ in majesty giving the keys to St Peter, who carries his pastoral crook (left), and receiving money from the donor of the church (right) – the figures defaced by iconoclasts. Excellent 15th-century N aisle and Langley Chapel. Very large barn s of the church with a steeply pitched roof, built c1200 probably by the Knights Hospitaller, who acquired the church shortly before.

**Slad** (B4) Like nearby Sheepscombe a village of cloth mills and weavers' cottages in a beautiful valley N of Stroud, and famous as the setting, in the early 1920s, of Laurie Lee's boyhood, described in his *Cider with Rosie:* 'Most of the cottages were built of Cotswold stone and roofed by split-stone tiles. The tiles grew a kind of golden moss which sparkled like crystallised honey . . . in the very sump of the valley wallowed the squire's Big House – once a fine, though modest, sixteenth-century manor, to which a Georgian façade had been added' – all of which is still true.

**Snowshill** (D7) perches decoratively on the side of a hill overlooking the Vale of Evesham. Snowshill Manor, 16th century with an early-18th-century classical entrance front and terraced gardens, now a National Trust property, houses large and eccentric collections of toys, clocks, musical instruments and domestic and farm implements amassed by its previous owner, Charles Wade, who spent part of his time here and the rest on his West Indian estates.

**South Cerney** (D3) Large rather sprawling village, now bordered s and E by the Cotswold Water Park. Large church with elaborate Norman s doorway, the arch surrounded by beakheads which become abstract shapes on the jambs. Hoodmould with frightening beast-heads for its stops. A narrow niche above the door contains carving in two layers, Christ in glory above, and the harrow-

*▼Lodge Park, 2 miles south-west of Sherborne, was built c1650 for John Dutton, who owned Sherborne House, as a pavilion from which to watch deer being coursed in the park: the balcony over the porch was the grandstand*

ing of hell below – virtually the mirror image of the harrowing over Quenington N door. The very beautiful 14th-century chancel has superbly carved sedilia (priests' seats) and piscina (basin for washing communion vessels). Late Norman tower arches leaning outwards give an almost Moorish look. Between them in a glass-fronted niche in the N wall is the church's greatest treasure, a wooden head and foot from a delicately carved 12th-century crucifix, formerly on the rood screen and found during restoration (1915) buried in the NE wall of the nave.

**Southrop** (E4) lies amid lush pastures in the Leach valley. Largely Norman church, tucked away behind the manor house (mostly 16th and 17th century, possibly of Norman origin) and almost part of its immaculate farmyard. S transept added c1300. Norman S doorway, under a late-14th-century porch, with diapered tympanum. Outstanding 12th-century sculptured font. John Keble lived at the Old Vicarage; ideas discussed with friends in this charming village later developed into the Oxford Movement.

**Stanton** (D7) Widely considered the most beautiful Cotswold village. The broad main street climbs the scarp slope towards Shenberrow Hill (site of an Iron Age fort) past the medieval village cross and carefully preserved cottages, all of local golden stone. At the E end of the village the gables of the manor house, 17th-century Stanton Court, are just visible over a high yew hedge. Opposite, one of the best-sited cricket pitches in the world gives fielders a view across the Vale of Evesham to Bredon Hill and beyond to the Malverns. The church has an elegantly proportioned 15th-century tower and spire and a carefully restored interior.

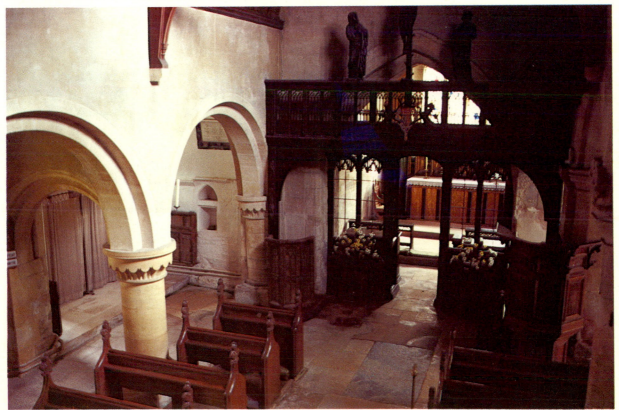

**Stanway** (D7), separated from Stanton by beautiful parkland dotted with oaks, is built of dark golden stone. The church and Stanway House with its elaborate Jacobean gateway, N of the village's thatched cottages, form one of the best-known architectural groups in the Cotswolds. The much-restored 12th-century church has a handsome 17th-century pulpit. A massive 14th-century tithe barn in the grounds of the House formerly belonged to the Abbot of Tewkesbury and is now the village hall.

**Stowell** (D5) A rather ponderous mansion (c1600), set in parkland, looks across the Coln valley to Chedworth woods. The church (behind the house, reached by walking up the drive from the steep narrow road along the park's N edge) is Norman, of cruciform shape, originally with a central tower. Five incised sundials on its s side; the one on the s transept window-sill may be Saxon. Late Norman crossing arch, with pretty rosettes carved on its capitals. Late-12th-century mutilated Doom painting on the nave N wall (Christ has disappeared from the top): the Virgin and apostles sit in elegant poses below a Romanesque arcade and watch with concern the sifting of souls, as angels and devils wait to collect their dues. The village, long since absorbed into the estate, is now no more than a few mounds in the park.

**Stow-on-the-Wold** (E6) Founded by the Abbey of Evesham c1050 to capitalise on a major crossing of routes between Warwick, Worcester, Gloucester and Malmesbury. Its exposed situation has no other advantage: 'Stow-on-the-Wold where the winds blow cold' is an accurate local saying. It quickly became a thriving market town, with two annual fairs by 1381; its horse fair (12 May) is still a regional event. Heavy traffic lessens Stow's potential charm but the

*▼ Stanway House (left), owned by the Earl of Wemyss and March, was built for the Tracy family 1580–1640 on the site of the Abbot of Tewkesbury's manor. The great bay window belongs to the hall. The elaborate gatehouse (right) was built c1630, probably to the design of a local mason*

market square, the best of any Cotswold town, remains unspoilt. Surrounded by traditional 16th- and 17th-century houses (except for the classical façade of 17th-century St Edward's House), it has, despite its size, a sense of courtyard-like enclosure enhanced by the evenness of the skyline and the unity of building materials. In this market square during the Civil War the last Royalist army was defeated, as Prince Rupert vainly attempted to check the Parliamentary advance on Gloucester. The church (mostly 13th century) was used to imprison the captured soldiers, and so badly damaged that it was declared ruinous — since when it has been restored three times.

**Stroud** (B4) An industrial town since the Middle Ages, the centre of the Cotswold cloth industry by 1500. Its chief advantage was the large supply of swift-flowing water in its steep valleys, necessary for fulling and for powering the mills. In the 1820s there were over 150 mills in the Frome valley (called 'golden' because of its wealth), almost threequarters of the total in the Cotswolds. Many survive, now converted to other uses; a very few still make fine cloth. Even during the industry's great depression in the 1830s Stroud went on producing cloth for the uniforms of most European armies: news that the Tsar had reviewed his troops in bad weather would cause all the weavers to get drunk on the promise of renewed employment, knowing that rain would stain the white tunics and new ones would be ordered. The imposing Stroud Subscription Rooms (1833), designed by George Basevi, with a ballroom occupying the whole first floor, and impressive classical Congregational Chapel (1835–7), designed by Charles Baker of Painswick, form a fine group and represent two important aspects of the early-19th-century industrial community — a newly rich middle class and the Nonconformist ethic. The parish church was entirely rebuilt 1866–8, except for its 14th-century tower. The late-16th-century Town Hall opposite forms one side of the narrow market place, which has a long cast-iron arcade for market stalls. Stroud's mixture of buildings of all styles and periods ranges from typical 17th- and 18th-century Cotswold clothiers' houses to terracotta-faced office blocks appropriate to London or a northern manufacturing city.

**Sudeley** (D6) once belonged to Ethelred the Unready. The last Lord de Sudeley, his descendant Ralph Boteler (succeeded 1398), was Admiral of the Fleet under Henry V and Henry VI, and with the proceeds of booty collected in the French wars he built Sudeley Castle. His surviving buildings are the gateway (1442), the Portmare Tower (named after the captured French admiral whose ransom financed it), St Mary's Chapel and the now ruined great tithe barn. In 1469 Boteler, being a Lancastrian, forfeited the castle to the new Yorkist king. The inner court was rebuilt, probably at the direction of Richard, Duke of Gloucester. The kitchen, dungeon tower, bay-windowed great presence chamber and Queen Katherine Parr's room date from this period. After Henry VIII's death his surviving wife, Katherine Parr, married Thomas, Lord Seymour of Sudeley (brother of Henry's third wife, Jane Seymour), and a year later died in childbirth at Sudeley. When Seymour was beheaded, following his attempt to marry his niece Lady Jane Grey to Edward VI, Sudeley passed to Thomas Brydges, who became 1st Lord Chandos of Sudeley in 1554. The 2nd Lord Chandos carried out the last major alterations, rebuilding the outer court (except the gatehouse) *c*1572; he entertained Elizabeth I here three times. During the Civil War the castle was used by Prince Rupert as a Royalist headquarters, and visited by Charles I after his failed attempt to capture Gloucester. It was successfully besieged (and badly damaged) in 1644 and became a Parliamentarian garrison. Lord Chandos, realising that the Royalist cause was lost, defected to Cromwell, but could not prevent the Parliamentarians from wrecking Sudeley (like Kenilworth Castle) as a safety measure. It remained a ruin until the 19th century, when the Dent family bought it with a fortune made in the gloving industry. As a result of their restoration and rebuilding the interiors are mostly 19th century but house good collections of furniture and works of art, notably (in the hall) outstanding paintings by Turner, Rubens, Ruysdael and Van Dyck and a superb Constable, *The Lock*. The gardens, laid out in the 19th century with formal yew hedges and parkland, are patrolled by vociferous peacocks. The ornamental pond is the last surviving fragment of Sudeley's moat.

**Swell** see **Lower Swell** and **Upper Swell**

**Swinbrook** (F5) Tiny village in the Windrush valley. A stream flows through the village green surrounded by farmhouses and cottages and overlooked by the church. Lord Redesdale came to live at Swinbrook after World War I. His daughter the novelist Nancy Mitford is buried in the churchyard, next to her sister Unity Valkyrie; the animal on her gravestone is the Mitford mole, which appears on the Redesdale coat of arms. The church, late Norman as the nave arcade shows, was enlarged in the 15th century with a clerestory and a big clear glass E window looking onto trees and meadows. Light streaming through it illumines the bizarre family monuments of the Fettiplaces' whose reclining effigies are stacked against the N chancel wall as though in bunk beds. The three on the left are Jacobean; those on the right, more relaxed and sophisticated, were added 1686. (The Fettiplaces' mansion was demolished in 1805, after the death of the last member of the family.) 15th-century choir stalls with carved misericords. Beautiful candlesticks and 18th-century chandeliers.

**Temple Guiting** (D6) Named after the Knights Templar, who had a community here. The village is hidden near the top of the Windrush valley in parkland and woods of beech, lime and oak, very different from the open exposed look of nearby Guiting Power. Approached from Kineton (s) the church and 18th-century Temple Guiting House form a fine group in a romantic situation. Church originally Norman, much altered in the 15th century, and again in the 18th when the Georgian windows were installed. Stained glass of c1500. Large handsome plaster coat of arms of George II (1742). 17th-century farms and cottages at Kineton. At Barton, ¾ mile down the valley and hemmed in by woodland, an 18th-century house and 17th-century farm overlook a pool, formerly a mill pond which supplied the first recorded fulling mill in England (1185) and now the haunt of coots. ½ mile further s, opposite the turn to Guiting Power, four massive gateposts make a monumental entrance to Guiting Stud Farm.

**Tetbury** (B3) Small market town with many good 18th-century clothiers' houses and several 17th- and 18th-century hotels and inns. In the early 19th century the coach trade replaced cloth as the main source of income, but within a few decades the railway had destroyed both the coach trade and the town's prosperity. In this century a constant flow of tourists has encouraged the numerous antique and tea shops, and the purchase of Highgrove House at nearby Doughton by the Prince and Princess of Wales has brought something of a boom.

▼ *Queen Katherine Parr's tomb in Sudeley church, which stands in the castle grounds. Henry VIII's surviving queen came to live at Sudeley Castle on her marriage to its owner, Thomas, Lord Seymour, and died there in childbirth in 1548. The church, financed by an earlier owner, Ralph Boteler, was built c1460 and damaged during the Civil War, when the castle was partially demolished. The interior was completely restored by George Gilbert Scott 1859–63. He designed the canopied tomb; the effigy was carved by J.B. Philip. The stained glass in the window behind is 13th century*

The Market House (1655) in the central market place, supported on three rows of squat columns, was probably designed for weighing wool. Tetbury's church was built 1781 after its medieval predecessor burnt down (the tower and spire survived but were rebuilt 1890), to designs by Francis Hiorn of Warwick. He may have been influenced by Warwick church, rebuilt after a fire in 1694; both have similarly spacious interiors, with aisles the same height as the lofty nave (the 'hall church' type), but this, as might be expected from its later date, is the more elegant, having exceptionally slender wood and iron columns, unusually large windows that flood the church with light, and a beautiful flat plaster vault. The gallery, box pews, brass chandeliers and gothick panelling are original. The altar painting is by Benjamin West, the American history painter favoured by George III. A wide corridor runs round the entire church with a door letting into each bay as though into a box at the theatre. A wall monument left of the s entrance has a famous inscription: 'In a vault under-neath/lie several of the Saunderses,/late of this parish: particulars/the last Day will disclose. Amen.'

**Thames and Severn Canal,** opened 1789, connected the Severn, via the Stroudwater Navigation, to the Thames at Lechlade. A spectacular piece of engineering, it included the longest canal tunnel then built, Sapperton Tunnel 2³/₈ miles). It was never a financial success: the Oxford Canal, opened only a year later, took much of its trade, and the porousness of the underlying limestone caused continual problems of water supply. It closed in 1933, leaving many traces, the most imposing being the tunnel portal near Coates (OS SP 966006). Above it is Tunnel House which, like Daneway Inn near Sapperton, served the bargees and leggers (who propelled the barges through the tunnel by thrusting their legs against the vault). The earth removed in the digging of air-shafts for the tunnel was made into little knolls and planted with beech trees, which now serve as waymarks along the tunnel from Daneway to Coates. The walk can be continued to Chalford along the old towpath through the thickly wooded valley. Unique to the Thames and Severn Canal are the five circular lengthsmens' houses for maintenance men, at Coates, Chalford (now a museum), Cerney Wick, Marston Meysey and Lechlade.

**Uley** (A3) Large 18th-century clothmaking village stretched along a hillside above the R. Cam, with many substantial clothiers' houses, notably round the green. Church rebuilt 1857–8. A tablet on the tower (too high to see properly) records the death (1731) of John Eyles, aged 90, 'the first that ever made Spanish cloth in this parish'. Spanish cloth or 'medleys', made from imported dyed Spanish wool, was introduced in an attempt to diversify after the slump in sales of white broadcloth, and its success led Cotswold clothiers to specialise in fine cloth dyed in a variety of colours. John Eyles' mill, 1 mile w at Wresden, is one of the oldest in Gloucestershire: a 16th-century house and, at the back, a small warehouse with round openings in the walls through which, it is thought, weavers handed in cloth and took out 'chains', bundles of wool to weave in their cottages.

Uley has two important prehistoric sites: Uleybury, a large Iron Age fort on the hill NW of the church, and, 1 mile N of the village, Hetty Pegler's Tump, a well-preserved Neolithic long barrow in the care of the Dept of the Environment and open to the public (w along path from B4066), named after the owner of the surrounding field, Hetty Pegler, who died in 1694.

**Upper Slaughter** (E6) Famous beauty spot. The road from the church crosses

►*Half of the astonishing double monument to the Fettiplace family in the chancel of Swinbrook church. This section was erected by Sir Edmund Fettiplace (died 1686); it was carved by William Bird, an Oxford sculptor who also did the carving on the Old Ashmolean Museum and the Sheldonian Theatre. To its left is another stack of three effigies, erected for an earlier Sir Edmund (died 1613); the vertical arrangement is dictated by the lack of space in this modest village church*

S[r]
EDMVND LETHPLACE
BARONET.

IN MEMORY OF
LETHPLACE
162[?]
Oxenfoote

the R. Eye through a ford. Cottages nestle into the tree-filled valley and have a withdrawn and private look. The church has a handsome small 15th-century pinnacled tower; its interior is mainly the result of restoration (1877). The mound E of it was the site of a castle, occupied 11th–13th centuries. Next to the churchyard and looking onto an open square are cottages remodelled by Lutyens. Upper Slaughter manor house – quintessential Tudor Cotswolds – was built for the Slaughter family on the site of a 15th-century priory, whose crypt survives and is haunted by the sound of ghostly children's laughter. Pretty terraced gardens full of roses.

**Upper Swell** (E6)  Attractive group of buildings set between a mill pond and the slope of the Dikler valley. 12th-century church. 16th-century manor house with an elaborate porch (1625) and landscaped grounds. Early-19th-century mill and water wheel. An 18th-century bridge spans the river.

**Westonbirt** (B2)  Largely 14th-century church with a tower above a baptistry on the s side. Westonbirt House (1863–70), designed by Vulliamy, a palace in Elizabethan style set in a huge park, is now a girls' school. Across the road is Westonbirt Arboretum, an outstanding landscaped collection of trees and shrubs – notably maples, rhododendrons and azaleas – cared for by the Forestry Commission and open to the public.

**Weston-sub-Edge** (D8)  Village on the border of the Cotswolds and the Vale of Evesham, reflecting both areas in its mixture of limestone and timber-framed buildings. Attractive 17th-century cottages in the main street. Heavily restored church with medieval tower.

► *Upper Slaughter: the medieval west tower of the church*

▼ *The massive portal of the Thames and Severn Canal (opened 1789) in Coates parish, beneath the Tunnel House Inn. This is the south-east end of Sapperton Tunnel (2.375 miles), the most ambitious canal tunnel that had yet been built*

**Whittington** (C6)  Church of Norman origin, s of the village's pretty cottages and set amidst the lawns of Whittington Court (16th century, on the site of an earlier house). Well-preserved 14th-century effigies of two knights and a lady confront the visitor who enters by the s door, their alarming effect enhanced by the knights' tense clutching of their swords.

**Winchcombe** (D6)  The most important town in the Cotswolds for much of the time between Cirencester's desertion by the Romans and its revival in the early Middle Ages, Winchcombe was the provincial capital of the kingdom of Mercia, controlling the n approaches to the wolds. King Coenwulf of Mercia founded a monastery here *c*798. His seven-year-old successor, Kenelm, was reputedly murdered whilst still a youth at the instigation of his ambitious sister. Her guilt was revealed when a scroll describing his burial place was dropped on the altar of St Peter's, Rome, by a dove which had flown from Kenelm's head at his death. Kenelm was buried in his father's monastery and his tomb became an important shrine, attracting pilgrims throughout the Middle Ages. At the Dissolution Thomas, Lord Seymour of Sudeley, bought the monastery and rased it to the ground. Two medieval stone coffins, said to be Coenwulf's and Kenelm's, discovered on its site in 1815, are preserved in the church nave. The church, sw of the monastery site, was built *c*1465, financed jointly by the monastery (the chancel) and the parish and Sudeley Castle (the nave) – the plainest of the Cotswold 'wool churches' but on a scale equal to them all (interior very thoroughly restored 1872–3). The parapet bears 140 boldly carved grotesque heads. The chief treasure is an altar cloth (behind a curtain left of the n door) made up in the 16th century from 14th-century priests' copes, incorporating the pomegranate emblem of Catherine of Aragon.

This handsome small town has excellent cream teas and varied examples of traditional Cotswold buildings, many with mansard roofs, a Winchcombe speciality. Jacobean House (1618), s of the church, formerly the grammar school, forms a good group with the Chandos Almshouses (1573) behind, financed by Lady Dorothy Chandos. Sudeley Almshouses (1865) are further E, a colourfully picturesque terrace by Sir George Gilbert Scott. Vineyard Street, the road to Sudeley, also has prettily terraced cottages and is lined with pollarded limes.

**Windrush** (E5)  Village spread up the slope of the Windrush valley opposite Barrington Park, with attractive cottages and houses round a triangular green. Beautiful and very well preserved church. The famous Norman s doorway is completely surrounded by a double row of beakheads, less sophisticated and varied than Elkstone's and all the more alarming. 12th-century elaborately decorated chancel arch. 15th-century timber roof resting on 12th-century grotesque corbel heads. A terminal on the N aisle arcade is carved into the shape of a sheep's head; there is also a sheep carved on one of the many splendid 18th-century table tombs in the churchyard.

**Winson** (D4)  Little village on the Coln between Bibury and Coln St Rogers. 17th-century and 18th-century cottages, classical manor house (c1740), small Norman church with excellent table tombs in the churchyard, and some good barns.

**Winstone** (C4)  Scattered farms in an exposed and remote situation on the uplands. The partly Saxon and partly Norman church, in open farmland, has a primitively barn-like interior. The utter simplicity of the Saxon N doorway contrasts with the diapered lintel and lozenge-patterned tympanum of the

▼ *Winchcombe High Street, one of the most attractively varied town streets in the Cotswolds. The half-timbered George Hotel was built for pilgrims to the shrine of St Kenelm; it bears the initials of a 16th-century abbot, Richard of Kidderminster, and has a splendid galleried courtyard*

Norman-influenced s doorway. The little saddle-backed tower is later.

**Withington** (D5) Large village on the Coln below Withington woods, with an 18th-century rectory, Tudor manor house and Norman church – the classic Cotswold combination. The church (its interior much altered in the 15th century) contains a marble monument to Sir John and Lady Howe (1651), shown in half-length effigies, with their eight children in relief. Their mansion at Cassey Compton, 1 mile E (D5), is an excellent example of the modification of traditional Cotswold architecture by the late-17th-century classical style.

**Woodchester** (B4), in the valley between Stroud and Nailsworth, reflects its clothmaking past in several 17th–19th-century mills and mill houses. Woodchester Park extends 2½ miles w; five lakes stretch along it. The house, designed by Benjamin Bucknall, was begun c1858 but never finished. Church 1863–4. Ruins of the abandoned Norman church lie at the N end of the village; just s of them is the site of the most magnificent Roman villa yet discovered in the Cotswolds, famous for its large and splendid mosaic pavement showing Orpheus charming the animals with his music. A protective covering of soil is cleared away about once every decade. At Wotton-under-Edge a replica is on permanent display, made, like the original, of cubes cut from local stones.

**Wotton-under-Edge** (A3) Market town in a valley incised into the Cotswold edge, sheltering under beechwoods. There was a market here in the 12th century, but according to tradition the town was destroyed in a fire started by King John's soldiers. In 1253 Lady Berkeley obtained a new grant of market and fair. Church consecrated 1283. Splendid late-14th-century tower. Gothick plaster ceilings c1800. Later restoration resulted in a dull interior. Large and beautiful tomb brasses of Thomas, Lord Berkeley (1417), and his wife Margaret (1392) (E end of N aisle). Thomas' father was reputedly the murderer of Edward

▲ *A detail of the early-14th-century wall-painting above the trefoiled sedilia in Hailes church. The owl, charming as it looks, has a sinister import: traditionally it is a bird of ill omen, and in its original state this painting showed it being attacked by the birds of light*

II at Berkeley Castle. His mother, Katherine, founded the grammar school, one of the oldest in England (1384), now in Gloucester Street in a building of 1726. The Berkeleys' manor house was replaced by The Manor (17th century) E of the church. In Church Street Perry's Almshouses (1632), founded by Hugh Perry of Wotton, who became Sheriff of London, are grouped in a little court-yard round a chapel. The chief accent of the High Street, which rises attractively up the hill, is the 18th-century façade of Tolsey House (formerly the market court), topped by a cupola and a dragon weathervane. Many of the best buildings date from the 17th and 18th centuries, when the cloth trade prospered. During its decline Wotton saw the worst unrest in the Cotswolds: in 1825 the clothiers' refusal to raise weavers' payment for cloth containing an increased number of threads led to a weavers' strike, which was successful only after riots in which several were killed and troops were called in. In Bear Lane, at the British School (1843), Isaac Pitman is thought to have begun the teaching of shorthand, a system he had devised at his home in Orchard Street. Edward Jenner (1749–1822), the discoverer of vaccination, was also a native of Wotton, and practised at Berkeley.

**Wyck Rissington** (E6), is in two groups: houses and farms around the church, and cottages surrounding a large green with a duckpond on the road to the Slaughters. The church, rebuilt 1269, comprises some of the best 13th-century architecture in the Cotswolds, notably the chancel and massive tower. In the E wall are two pairs of tall narrow lancets, each topped with a lozenge-shaped window with concave sides, and, at the apex, a straight-sided lozenge window, all drawn together by a continuous string-course. The chancel, with a medieval rafter roof, has fragments of 14th-century stained glass, including a crucifix in the S window. Gustav Holst was organist and choirmaster here – his first professional post.

**Yanworth** (D5) The 12th-century church, surrounded by large barns a little way from the village, seems to belong to a farmyard. Late Norman S doorway. The tower arch's N pier has a 16th-century wall-painting of Death, a skeleton with a scythe(?), shroud and sexton's shovel. Vigorous carved corbel heads support the nave and N transept roofs.

# THE COTSWOLDS

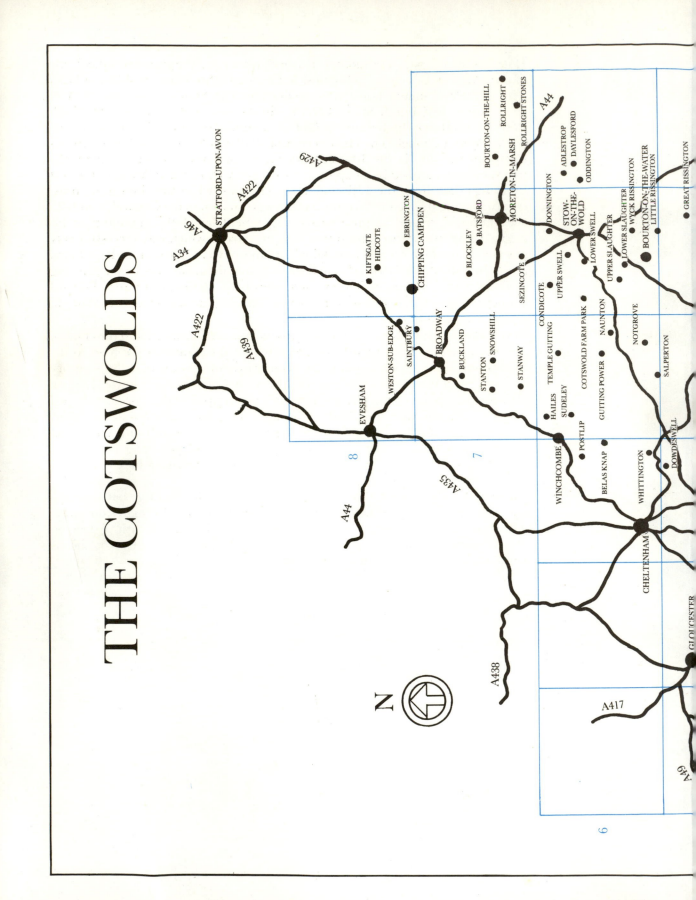